From

Touched

to

Exalted

N A N C Y   J O N E S

ISBN 978-1-64299-320-2 (paperback)
ISBN 978-1-64299-353-0 (hardcover)
ISBN 978-1-64299-321-9 (digital)

Christian Faith Publishing, Inc.
832 Park Avenue
Meadville, PA 16335
www.christianfaithpublishing.com

Printed in the United States of America

Contents

Exalted

Foreword

REVEREND DAVID F. KELLER

Learn about Nancy's incredible journey. From her own experience she has recognized there are countless wounded adults from traumatic childhoods that are spiritually bankrupt and void of any hope for change as she once was. Based upon the many institutions that have eliminated a positive concept it's no wonder there appears to be no possibility of healing.

There are those, like Nancy, who believe they carry the responsibility to present to skeptics and non-believers the "idea" of a healing personal relationship rather than a restrictive organized religious genre. People who have tested this relationship may be the only catalyst toward true love and faith.

Nancy's story begins with unimaginable neglect, physical and emotional abuse, and repeated abandonment. Love and trust were painfully absent. From attempted suicide as a teenager to decades of counseling, 12 Step programs, metaphysical energy healing, bodywork, reading of innumerable self-help books and acupuncture she succeeded in recognizing the numerous issues that contributed to her need for something more.

Nancy graciously recognizes that for such a time as this people of all ages are desperate for hope instead of fear; love instead of hate and trust instead of deceit. Allow her to share with you her transformation from occasional spiritual touches to the most important relationship ever as well as wholeness in mind, body and spirit.

Introduction

Approximately thirty years ago the Lord touched me and implanted a dream in my spirit that I would someday write a book. He went even further and gave me the title *From Touched to Exalted*. My personal interpretation of this title reminded me of the many times in my life when I had a distinct awareness that God himself had touched me in a particular situation and made a way to rise above the said situation and thus be exalted. As I share my journey in the following pages I trust you will be encouraged to contemplate and perhaps record the instances in your life that have presented themselves as touches from God. When I shared my vision of writing a book with a dear friend that I jointly taught a lunchtime Bible study with, he was elated and asked me if I would honor him by having him write the foreword to the said book. I was so inspired I wrote and submitted an article to a Christian magazine that was graciously rejected. This incident discouraged me to the point that I dismissed myself from following through with what I surmised I had mistakenly heard from God. I realize today how totally ridiculous I was to give up after one attempt at having something published!

At times we, as believers, who have not yet grown to act on things by faith are easily discouraged. Subsequently, I continued my career as a phone company employee quite successfully. However, on more occasions than I can count people commended me regarding notes I had written in greeting cards and personal letters. They told me that those writings were keepsakes for them because they had been so blessed by them. These comments aroused me in my spirit as I acknowledged them as "nudges" from God that encouraged me to again attempt to pursue writing as one of His personal gifts to me.

There were a very few trusted friends that I felt comfortable sharing my dream of writing a book, but for the most part it was a well-kept secret. Occasionally friends would ask me if I had started my book and I would humbly respond that I still had the intention. As the years went by the awareness that I had a gift for writing as well as speaking became more evident. In 2005, as I shared a writing at a small support group, the leader informed me of a friend who helped people get their books published. Almost immediately afterward another trusted friend reminded me that she had a degree in journalism and would be delighted to edit whatever I wrote! Still I procrastinated based on my fear of failure. I suppose what finally convinced me that God was nudging even harder was when I shared my dream at a Bible based book study and a young man said he would love to read any writing project of mine even if I chose not to publish it. I received his comment as an immensely direct encouragement from God.

As I began to earnestly and specifically pray about my proposed book God literally gave me two scriptures that were previously noted and highlighted in my favorite Bible from July 1978 when I was faced with a major life decision The first passage was Ezekiel 38:14 that reads, "I will put my Spirit in you, and I will place you in your own land; then you will know that I, the Lord, have spoken it and performed it, says the Lord." My interpretation of that passage this time was that the Lord would place and favor me again according to His will for me and that I would know that He had acted on my behalf. The second scripture was Romans 11:29 in which God said to his servant Paul, "The gifts and calling of God are without repentance." I had noted in my Bible that when God calls us for something He does not change His mind!

I know Our God is so faithful and personal to His children but it still continues to amaze me as I experience His work being done in me. In the summer of 2007 God reminded me that at age fifteen I had won a writing contest in which I competed with students from several Western Pennsylvania suburban high schools. That remembrance was more confirmation in my spirit that God had planted the seed for me to write. Soon afterward I was led to a sermon I had taken notes on about the year 2008 being the year for fullness of God's blessings by way of new beginnings. The scriptures were Romans 15:29 and Isaiah 42:9. In Romans Paul refers to his confidence in the upcoming perilous journey that he would be making to Jerusalem, Rome, and Spain to speak to the Gentiles. He declared, "I know that when I come to you I will come in the full measure of the blessing of Christ." With that passage I felt assured that God wanted me to take it personally that He would bring me into the fullness of His purpose for me. In Isaiah 42:9 the Lord gave His prophet the following, "See, the former things have taken place, and new things I declare; before they spring into being I announce them to you." My personal interpretation of this passage was the blessings He had bestowed on me needed to be declared, and He would continue to let me know His direction in my new endeavor of sharing my testimony with others verbally and in a future published book.

I certainly wondered why I had to previously endure so many hardships in my life. I've come to believe God's greatest blessings often come from hard times and then comes the fullness of His plan and purpose. I'm reminded of my childhood years which were much less than desirable and left me emotionally wounded, but nevertheless God has blessed me mightily in my adult years as I grew in my personal relationship with Him. Satan may have meant those experiences for irreversible evil but God turned them into good. One thing I've learned for sure through my many life experiences is when Satan turns up the notch to dissuade us God turns up a stronger one as is written in I John 4:4 that reads, "The one is in you is greater than the one who is in the world."

I'm reminded just now of a sermon I heard around this time in which the pastor made a statement that hit me like a sledgehammer. The Lord said to him (and subsequently to me), "Do you think I've brought you this far, with so many blessings, for you to keep it to yourself?" The sermon continued with examples of men of faith that God had certainly blessed and used mightily, but they somehow stepped out of God's will and purpose. The examples in God's Word are numerous such as Moses, David, Samson, and many others. What's important for us as believers is we be assured that God blesses those he calls with power, knowledge, ability, strength, and anything else needed to fulfill His purpose for us.

Join me as I share my life journey thus far from being touched through many devastating experiences, to be exalted above them all by God's love, grace, and faithfulness. I'm quite certain many of you who have prepared to read this memoir have unrevealed stories that burden you spiritually, emotionally, and even physically. I have finally come to really believe what Jesus said to those who follow Him, that the "truth will set you free" (John 8:32) and the more truth we reveal the more we heal.

It is my prayer that these memories I've recorded serve as encouragement to others, young and old, to seek God for the wholeness in mind, body, and spirit spoken of in 1 Thessalonians 5:23.

Beginnings

Chapter 1

Earliest Conditions

The following is written as I imagine what my mother, myself, and others might have contemplated as I grew in the womb. There was a strong sense of uncertainty regarding an unwanted pregnancy out of wedlock. Mixed emotions presented themselves as my mother pondered the fantasies of motherhood compared to the resentment created by the abrupt change in her plans for further education.

Did I experience a fear of rejection even then as I considered how others would respond to my birth circumstances? Is anyone really happy that I'm going to be born? Today there exists scientific proof that babies in utero actually experience a certain amount of comprehension and some of that gathered information prepares them for the outside world. Further research indicates babies actually develop some senses especially during the last trimester. "What Babies Learn in the Womb" (parenting.com).

My father felt stuck, confused, and bewildered; complacent rather than overjoyed. I've gathered information that strongly suggests his basic thoughts were, "Well I guess I'll just have to deal with it if she says the baby's mine. My mama doesn't believe the baby's mine and I have to deal with that also but she's going to stick around to help." My paternal grandma was unbelieving and skeptical about my upcoming birth. She thought her son was stupid to take on the responsibility of marriage and fatherhood but she resolved to make the best of it and continue to live at her current residence with the addition of a daughter-in-law and a child.

Others who knew the details of the situation were awaiting the outcome of the illegitimate pregnancy, the shotgun wedding and new living arrangements. My father was the youngest of four sons and had just returned from a tour in the army with intentions of staying at home with his mother who had been a widow for several years. Based on several circumstances it was agreed that my father would continue to reside with his mother and my mother would simply move in. There was no chance that my mother could have lived with her father and stepmother because she had literally escaped the household and the dysfunction thereof by tying bedsheets together and climbing from a second floor window. She was temporarily staying with an older brother and his family. Marriage to my father seemed like a better option so she agreed to move in after marriage. My father was considered a good catch from a Christian family, at least before he went overseas with the US Army. No one really knew what worldly habits he had acquired during his two years of service overseas in Germany and France. The maternal grandparents were basically relieved to not be responsible for their daughter and baby and thus would not have to explain or endure the embarrassment of a daughter with an illegitimate child.

My early childhood years are quite vague. For some reason I don't personally have any pictures myself and the one that I remember pictured me as a little girl but with a strangely solemn facial expression. I've mostly depended on other family members and friends to relate the events and stages I went through.

Mom, Dad and Me 1947

I do remember spending time with my paternal grandfather and stepgrandmother. I remember the house being immaculate and my having many restrictions as a visiting grandchild. Little to no affection was received from my stepgrandmother but I recall my grandfather working puzzles with me and teaching me gardening skills. My most favorite remembrance is how often we had ice cream treats from a freezer with several choices. It seemed at the time that I was the only grandchild that spent two to three days with my grandfather even though there were several other grandchildren from my mother's siblings. My grandfather was an active member at a local United Methodist church that I attended often. Those visits often were with my mother who had an amazing voice and sang at various programs. Around five years old I began to play little piano selections at those same events and remember my mother and grandfather expressing great pride as I did so.

In my toddler and very young ages I'm told my mother presented me as the cutest, smartest, best dressed, and talented child ever! Unfortunately, I have little to no memories of those gratifying events. It seems as though even then my sense of worth was based upon what I did rather than who I was. In retrospect I was probably being labeled with these characteristics to validate my legitimacy in spite of my birth circumstances. I have a few fond memories of visiting a local dairy store with my mom and getting an ice cream cone. Many years later in my adulthood I recognized that ice cream had became a comforting substance that unfortunately demonstrated love and affection to me and eventually became my drug of choice. At the height of my adult compulsive eating career I regularly consumed a gallon of ice cream a day (usually in the evenings) to satisfy my distorted emotions that were a huge part of my existence.

I also have numerous wonderful recollections of my paternal grandmother who lived with us in my early childhood years. She didn't demonstrate a lot of touchy-feely affection perhaps because she had four sons. However, her love was certainly apparent as she taught me to be a little helper, mostly in the kitchen, when meals were prepared two to three times daily. Upon reflection I recognize those cooking experiences as further demonstrations of what I considered love well into my adult years. She also taught me to iron handkerchiefs and underwear at a very young age. The most lasting skill she taught me was how to sew by hand and on a treadle sewing machine long before I could even work the pedal myself.

I have very few memories of affection shown me by my father during my early childhood. He never seemed to be a loving person and had the reputation of being a huge angry man. He never, however, abused me and seldom physically punished me compared to my mother who did the direct opposite, and physically punished me and my brother for almost anything.

CHAPTER 2

Normal Family Life

My recollection of ages six to ten is filled with turmoil. I became painfully aware of the realities in my family situation and unpleasant doesn't begin to describe the emotional unrest that was so damaging. It became very obvious that my parents were unhappily married and basically angry about each other. Alcohol consumption became a severe problem and was accompanied by arguing and fighting on a regular basis. On many occasions we visited relatives' houses where the main events were drinking and gambling. Many times those visits ended with arguing, loud obnoxious cursing, and accusations of cheating undoubtedly resulting from the large amounts of alcohol consumed.

Our "family outings" were often to the local "after hour" joints where my brother and I would be placed in a booth with sodas and chips. Our parents frequented these same places quite often without us and I would remain sleepless worrying if the night would end with arguing and fighting once they returned home.

For some unknown reason at the time my mother would become nastily boisterous and continue relentlessly until my father would respond by eventually beating her with his huge fists. For explanation's sake let me tell you again that my father was very large in stature and unquestionably strong. On the other hand, my mother was a short woman of medium stature so it didn't take much to knock her down. To this very day I can't bear to watch even boxing scenes as they arouse vivid memories of my mother being punched, knocked to the floor, and bleeding profusely.

My brother and I, as well as my grandmother, would all sit in absolute terror worrying if one of those fights would end fatally. Actually there was one particular incident where my father had kicked or thrown my mother down a flight of stairs onto a concrete basement floor and immediately left the house, perhaps fearing he had killed her. I will never forget looking down at her with blood running from her mouth and her body motionless. Grandma hesitantly started down the steps first with me clinging to her arm and Doug clinging to me. After what seemed like at least five to ten minutes we gasped big sighs of relief when Mommy moved and began moaning before we reached the bottom of the stairs.

During these same years my mother chose to leave home for months at a time and participate in extramarital relationships. At times my brother and I were given the opportunity to spend weekends with my mother and her current friend only to frequent even more bars in the city. Our sleeping arrangements were in rented rooms sometimes with or without the benefit of a second bed or a sofa so we slept on the floor. Very sadly these affairs always ended with similar results considering the combination of alcohol and physical fighting. For still unknown reasons my father would go to hospitals or jails to rescue my mother and take her home until her next venture away from home and her children.

On many occasions my grandmother would try to intercede by asking my mother to be quiet and her son to stop beating her. Seemingly never accomplishing any results, she would sit down on her bed and begin to pray and hum hymns that I perceived at the time as doing nothing. To add to the confusion, my mother would often scream for me to call or go get the police. Many times our phone service happened to be disconnected at the time or I was afraid to go downstairs to use it. More times than I can count I would climb out the second floor window, walk across the roof, shimmy down an oak tree, and run to the police station two blocks away.

As I think about these frequent incidences (often weekly) I find it ironic that we lived next door to a police chief who never chose to intervene even if he was at home. Other neighbors certainly heard the commotion coming from our house but they, too, did not call the police. When the police did respond they would simply ask my father to leave the house rather than take him to jail. I suppose they were lenient with him because he worked for the borough as a street sweeper operator and was generally liked. Many times after the police came and left my mother would physically abuse me for actually getting them. Imagine the mixed emotions and confusion I experienced having summoned the police to come after my father, who had been totally pushed to extreme anger, and my mother's cries for help. Describing these events as horrible only scratches the surface of the extreme trauma my brother and I experienced and were consequently wounded in our spirits for years.

Many times my father left the house rather than beat my mother. She would then be physically, verbally, and emotionally abusive to my brother and me for absolutely no reason and sometimes for hours until she fell asleep in a drunken stupor. To add to my traumatized thoughts sometimes I actually agreed with some of the punishing blows my father initiated based on the terrible things my mother would be shouting.

One of the most devastating results of my mother's drunken abuse was the night she literally pushed and shoved my grandmother down the stairs and out of the house. Afterward she proceeded to throw my grandmother's belongings out the window. My grandmother never returned to live with us even during the times my mother left for months at a time. I'm certain my grandmother loved us but was just too old to continue to be exposed to the abuse, neglect, and violence in our domestic situation. She would come and visit when she knew my mother was absent and taught me many household chores as well as cooking.

A blessing in our childhood was my mother's sister Lella and her husband Melvin. Even though they had five children of their own in a small three-bedroom apartment they would often take Doug and me for weekends. Today I have more appreciation than ever for them because I know the level of responsibility that is required raising, feeding, and clothing their own children, much less adding two more. During the times my mother was living at home, one or two of Aunt Lella's and Uncle Melvin's children would visit us. For the most part those were somewhat times of relief because my mother would not be as outwardly abusive or get as falling down drunk. What was especially confusing was my observation of how my mother treated my younger girl cousin Sharon who often came to visit for a few days. By comparison to myself, she was treated like a little china doll and I became a raggedy Ann slave to her.

Aunt Lella and Uncle Melvin

The fighting and arguing between my mother and father became a family secret that none of her siblings seemed to talk about. The few times I managed the courage and trust to desperately attempt discussion with one of my uncles or Aunt Lella I was immediately told not to speak about what happens in our household. The black eyes, busted lips, and disfigured nose were evidence of what was happening but my brother and my accounts were immediately squelched. The minimal talk I overheard indicated that my father was the villain and my mother was an undeserving victim.

CHAPTER 3

More Reality

Gas and electric utilities were often disconnected for weeks or months at a time. When the gas was off we cooked on an electric hot plate. There seemed little need to hurry and pay the gas bill during summer months. When the electricity was shut off there was a more expedient effort to get it turned back on. There was no bathroom in the house, only a toilet in the dirt basement that usually only flushed by dumping buckets of water into it. The alternative to a commode was the use of metal cans with lids that would be emptied into the basement toilet. That particular chore became even more disgusting as one tried to scare away the rats that had permanent residence in the said basement. There was an outhouse in our backyard for years. When we could water was heated on the gas stove or an electric hot plate and poured into a large aluminum tub for bathing. Finally the Board of Health was notified and our landlord was forced to install a bathroom.

In addition to the nightly fear of domestic violence my brother and I often had difficulty sleeping as we heard rats scampering across the bedroom floor or inside the walls. It was always a frightening experience to be ordered to go downstairs to the kitchen after dark and hear or see the rats running for cover. There were countless times we were summoned to go downstairs for a beer from the refrigerator or to make a bologna sandwich no matter what time of night or early morning hour it was. Having food in the house was hit or miss. If it had not been for the welfare food distributions we often would have little to no food in the house. As the oldest child I was delegated to go and stand in line for the free food that consisted of such things as peanut butter, powdered milk, canned meat, oatmeal, lard, butter, cheese, and flour. A great treat was to have the meat that resembled pulled pork with homemade biscuits if we had baking powder to make the biscuits and the gas was on. I actually remember going to neighbor houses to ask for a tablespoon of baking powder.

In all fairness I must say that the times my mother lived with us for a few weeks or months at a time the food situation was definitely better. Those times were great because there was an effort expended to have things appears as if all was well. However, as my mother's alcoholism progressed and her absences became more frequent good meals were few and far between unless we were expecting a visit from extended family members. For some unknown reason my parents were considered perhaps middle income and further up the poverty scale than others in the family.

My father would frequently have poker games at our house that were always loud and my brother and I became the wait service for food, beer, and shots. One particular night there was an attempted shooting where the bullet just missed my brother's head as we peeked from the stairway to observe the awful disturbance. My father held these games and took a portion of each winning hand for "the house."

One would think that we would have been better provided for with my father gainfully employed and the extra income from his poker games. Wrong! His other glaring fault was playing illegal numbers. Whereas other households had rent, utilities, food, and clothing as family priorities my father's first and foremost payment was his illegal numbers bill. Our clothing consisted entirely of hand-me-downs from the families my mother did housework for. Even when she wasn't living with us she would stop by and leave clothes for us. One might think that was a good thing but children can be extremely cruel. My brother and I were ridiculed when those two colored kids showed up in school with clothes on that were recognized as previously owned. We were teased unmercifully. To this very day I take the greatest of pride in how I'm able to dress based on the adverse clothing conditions of my young childhood.

The previously mentioned dynamics continued but even more neglect and abuse developed. My father decided to let a senior man come to live with us who was an absolute alcoholic. Unfortunately I became the object of sexual molestation from this man on several occasions even though penetration was not possible. I remember feeling there was something very wrong with what he was doing to me but had no idea what to do to stop it. An amazing amount of shame enveloped me in addition to the fear he instilled in my young mind that if I did tell anyone I would be in great trouble. He had me convinced that anyone I told would conclude what was happening to me was my fault and I would be labeled a very bad person like my mother and punished harshly by my father. I couldn't even bring myself to tell my grandmother who no longer lived with us but was a short walk away for me to visit.

Around the same period of time I experienced molestation from one of my mother's friends while visiting her for the weekend. My mother had gone downstairs to get something from the kitchen that she had access to. Said friend came and sat next to me on the sofa bed and reached under my dress and into my panties. I immediately hollered as loudly as I could for my mother. When she entered the room I ran to her, hugged her and told her what had happened. To my total shock my mother punched me around my mouth and called me a liar! She then told me to pack my few things because she was sending me home. As we left the one-room apartment and headed for the bus stop we had to walk down a very steep hill. As we proceeded down the hill my mother repeatedly pushed and shoved me to the point that I had to keep catching myself to keep from falling forward. Once we reached the bus stop she called my father on a pay phone and told him I had lied and accused her friend of something he would never do. She went on to say that I should be punished when I arrived home. Of course I cried all the way home and experienced even more devastation when my father scolded me for lying and sent me to my room. He seemed not to even consider asking me what had happened. This incident, in addition to what had happened with my father's boarder, instilled some strong feelings of total abandonment and hopelessness that only continued to become greater and more persistent as time went by.

My self-esteem was totally in the gutter and I concluded that I was being punished by the wrathful God my Baptist minister spoke about. In my thoughts I was a terrible sinner for hating both my mother and father and these things that were happening to me were God's anger pouring down on me.

During my early teen years my mother labeled me "a big ugly black bastard." Every time she spoke those horrible words they seemed to rip a part of my heart away and become engrained in my mind. I did have a large frame and was always the first or second kid in lines during gym classes. There were also some very distorted parameters among people of color that exist to this day. Those of us with darker complexions were considered "less than" on the scale of human value. Yes, this terrible concept originated during slavery times, but remains a very strong element imposed by people of color and Caucasians. Lighter complexion folks were held in a little higher esteem and were actually treated differently. Just living and breathing with my darker complexion generated constant not okay feelings and added to my low self-esteem. Only a few years ago as I began to acknowledge my truths and talk about them did I realize that African-American people with a lighter complexion experienced these very same not okay feelings because their ancestors were conjugated with Caucasians and therefore labeled as half-breeds among other names. Their label became yellow people and they, too, were denigrated for not being authentically "black." Today I know that people of all ethnicities suffer condemnation from others who are not the same. Those inferior feelings can last a lifetime and present a constant emotional struggle. Feelings of adequacy and equality can become totally nonexistent in the minds of such emotionally damaged people. These negative self-impressions can be brutal and affect every other area of one's existence no matter how successful they might become in adulthood. I've even come to the conclusion that after struggling with extreme emotional brokenness for decades the results eventually begin to take a toll on one's physical health even to the point of mental illness, death, addiction, or suicide.

CHAPTER 4

Teen Years and Trouble

By the time I turned thirteen I realized that as the oldest child in a home with alcoholism, abuse, and neglect I assumed the role of the responsible child. I started filling in for my mom at the homes where she did housekeeping. Even though I worked as hard as an adult and did a very substantial job, I was paid as if I was a child. Most times the money I did make had to be used to buy food for my brother and myself.

A very confusing dilemma presented itself when I dared to mention the terrible things that were happening within our house during the times my mother was living there. None of her siblings would listen to my complaints about the abuse I was encountering. It was total invalidation of my truths and attempts at expressing my emotions. Their constant response was, "That's your mother and you are to *never* talk negatively about her." The consequences of those responses resulted in my learning to suppress and repress my emotions even more, not to mention slight facial responses just for grimacing at some abusive statement my mother made to me. In addition, I dare not display any signs of pain or even think about crying. Many comedians joke about parents disciplining them and immediately telling them to "shut up" but that actually happened to me and it certainly wasn't funny at the time. Imagine building up such a tolerance to pain that in adulthood doctors and other health professionals comment on how "well" we endure pain.

I'm quite certain my aunt and uncles knew exactly what was going on in our household and the victimization my brother and I were forced to suffer through. They seemed to ignore the scars and marks on our bodies. There was never any mention of my mother's lengthy absences and affairs that my brother and I were exposed to. Nor was there mention of the many times my father would rescue her from those inappropriate encounters. To this day I fail to have any understanding of what prompted my father to continue those rescues. Only as I started mentioning my intentions to write this memoir was I told that one of my uncles had inquired about adopting me.

At age fifteen life tribulations seemed to close in on me. My mother and I did not get along at all and I became more of a victim of verbal abuse. The reality of that situation was the two or three months "visits" of my mother's interfered with the position of head of household that had been forced on me during her many absences. We both resented each other and she began to tell vicious lies to my father about things she "heard' I was doing. It appeared my father believed the falsehoods and I was no longer favored by him even though there were never any demonstrations of affection from him, not even hugs unless I initiated them on rare occasions. I had a sense that he at least cared about me but I began to feel abandoned even by him and it appeared that there was no reason to continue living life as I knew it.

One night that my mom was particularly evil after drinking and being beaten by my father (who left) it became my turn for more verbal and physical abuse. I gave thought to hitting her myself since I was bigger than her, but had a change of mind and left the house around 3:00 AM and headed for the church where I thought I could at least talk to the God I heard a few trustworthy church people speak about. Much to my chagrin the doors to the church were locked! My conclusion about being locked out even from God's presence (that I thought was only in the church) I began to cry hysterically for what seemed like hours. Around dawn I noticed a light go on in what seemed like the kitchen of a house next door to the church. A few moments later a police car pulled up and the chief approached me. I thought for sure he would take me away to a juvenile facility like my brother had been placed in. My opinion was at least I would be away from the turmoil in my daily life. The police chief was more than familiar with the circumstances in my family. He invited me into the car and began discussion with me that I will never forget.

He began by saying, "You're a very smart and nice young girl who is well liked by your peers and others in this community. My wife and I have discussed how you've remained such a good kid with all that goes on in your family. You need to recognize that in just two short years you will be eighteen years old and can do and be whatever you choose. Just try to hang in there until then." His conversation encouraged me, but only until the next fit of rage that was directed at me. My mother chose to spread the word that I was out all night with an older teenage boy the night I spent on the church steps. I contemplated trying to have the police chief contact my father and tell him what really happened but I knew that for some unknown reason my mother would move on to yet another lie concerning my character. At this point I admitted at least to myself that I really hated my mother and yet I was ashamed of that intense feeling.

In the midst of that same summer Marilyn Monroe was found dead and it was reported as suicide. As an extremely impressionable teenager I concluded that if a beautiful, rich, successful white woman found no reason to live, surely I had none either. At that time I gathered my thoughts and concluded I was the lowest of the low class citizens in my small town. No matter how I tried to rise above said feelings I still carried a mountain of shame around my appearance and my family issues. At that particular moment I had totally negated what the police chief had told me and decided to take my life.

I went to the local grocery store and stole a bottle of sleeping pills. When I returned home a neighbor was sitting on her back porch as she often did and I spoke to her in a mannerly fashion. I went inside the house and took the entire bottle of pills. I laid across my bed with little to no remorse and a greater sense of relief that my struggle as a "big ugly black bastard" was over! Sometime later my grandmother "happened" to decide to visit the neighbors to chat and perhaps check on me if I happened to be home. During conversation my grandmother mentioned that it looked as if no one was home in our house. The neighbor proceeded to tell my grandmother that she had seen me go into the house a while ago. What prompted my grandmother to come into the house and upstairs was that I didn't answer her calls. She, of course, found me on the bed and saw the empty pill bottle. Only God knew I had made this suicide attempt and I will believe until the day I die that He sent my grandma there at that very time to save my life! She accomplished this by making a mixture of powdered Cheer laundry detergent and water. She subsequently made me bend over our nasty toilet and force me to drink glass after glass of that horrible tasting mixture. I felt the need to regurgitate several times. To this very day just my thoughts of that product produces a queasy stomach and a nauseous taste in my mouth even as I write these words! *Ugh!* Needless to say, I've never bought Cheer and even try not to look at it on grocery shelves.

Grandma Scates

In retrospect I know today that God cared for me more than I cared for myself. I wasn't even grateful that I was still alive. Later my grandmother sat down beside me and had these words to say, "You must keep this incident a total secret. If you don't you will be put in a place like your Uncle Buck where there are crazy people. Those are the kind of people that try to take their lives and you don't want to live in a mental hospital for the rest of your life. You need to keep doing well in school, graduate, and get a good job to live by yourself until you get married." Grandma was referring to her son that had become afflicted with syphilis during his time in the army that affected his mental capacity.

My response to Grandma was, "Will you come live with me?"

She said as she so often did, "If it's God's will."

REFLECTION

Today I have come to realize that the suicide rate among adult children of alcoholics is extremely high. Very often if the self-destruction is not suicide it's some other form of self-abuse such as alcohol, food, drugs, and even sex. Later as you read more about my life journey you'll find I actually came to a point that I thanked God for my addiction to food/sugar. He didn't cause it, but my drug of choice could have been much worse. My brother's addiction was drugs that led him to a very tragic death. Even though I struggled for decades from my abusive childhood I managed to cling even to the slightest hope that there really was a God and that I could someday be acceptable to Him. My brother made a different choice but I still have much love and compassion in my soul for him as he struggled without that same measure of hope. It is certainly my prayer that God himself will open the eyes of those who read this testimony and recognize the difference a relationship with Him matters.

―≈≈≈―

At age sixteen along comes what any teenager would consider love. I met and started dating the brother of Aunt Lella's best friend during a summer I spent with them. Imagine having someone even act like I was someone special! In my confused mind the physical consequences of that yearlong relationship were necessary to "prove my love." I can even remember the weekend I gave into physical desires because it was the same weekend that our President John F. Kennedy was assassinated! I still remember the shock and desolation I experienced from that devastating event. For those of you that expected me to omit my teenage shortcomings that will not be happening. Too often nowadays older adults (especially Christians) conveniently develop selective amnesia when it comes to the things they did as teenagers and young adults. I choose not to do that because young people need to be made aware that those of us who have come to know and love the Lord in our later years often came with a multitude of sins. We older adults do a great disservice to our young people by not sharing many of our truths with them. Sharing these stories with them could seemingly provide encouragement and hope to those who feel they are incapable of receiving God's total forgiveness and unconditional love.

I know for a fact that God has totally forgiven me and it was only by his grace that I wasn't punished for my mishaps. I distinctly remember how I started retail theft as a young teenager in local grocery stores so that my brother and I would have food to eat. I didn't make enough money cleaning houses to adequately provide for us. Most times my father looked to me to furnish meals and he never asked where the food came from. I'm quite sure the managers and employees at those local stores knew that I was stealing but perhaps chose to show some compassion because they somehow knew the family situation. I wonder even if they summoned the police and the officers chose to ignore my thefts.

One Christmas Eve I was extremely disappointed that we had no tree. My resolve to that dilemma was to investigate stealing one. I stealthily waited until approximately midnight when I presumed the people that were selling trees a few blocks away would certainly be gone and they were. I actually picked a very nice tree that I could carry on my back and began the trek back to the house. Wouldn't you know I became aware of a car following slowly behind me. When I gathered enough nerve to see who was following me in that vehicle I was shocked beyond measure to discover that it was a police car! I immediately began to imagine myself being hauled off to jail and quickly began to conjure up a lie that I had paid for the tree. To my total amazement, in what seemed like an eternity, the car continued up the hill away from me. Imagine me then running as fast as I possibly could toward home crying all the way with combined emotions of joy for not being confronted by the police and shame that I had stolen a tree that was a symbol of a holy holiday.

I graduated to retail theft of clothing at a shopping center outside of Oakmont and was not as fortunate. When I was caught the police from that locality called the Oakmont police to come and pick me up. As I rode in the back of that police car I actually prayed that God would let me die because I knew my father would surely kill me. The Oakmont policeman took me into the jailhouse and into a cell! As I looked at the commode and sat on the cot I imagined myself in this setting for years. After what seemed like hours the chief came into the cell and once again spoke with me. I distinctly remember him saying, "Well, young lady, once again you're in trouble and it's much more serious this time. What you've done today could ruin your chances for the successful life we spoke about." Of course by this time I thought I would surely have a heart attack and drop over dead my heart was pounding so severely. He continued saying, "I've spoken to some other people here in the community including your pastor and have decided not to tell your father what you've done." At that point I thought for sure I was dreaming and not really hearing what he had said. He continued, "We're going to let you leave by the back entrance and we'll not mention this incident to anyone else. However, we cannot promise you that a criminal file will not be established by the other police establishment. Needless to say, if you repeat any theft at all and are caught you will be institutionalized for a long time."

The guilt and shame from that incident was overwhelming to say the least and I had nightmares for weeks afterward. Today, I know it was truly the grace of God that delivered me from this incident. Even though I had many doubts regarding His existence, I know that He was there at that time for sure.

CHAPTER 5

My Dear Brother

I would be quite remiss if I didn't take the time to speak of my dear brother. If I felt my prenatal condition was horrendous my brother's was absolutely life-threatening and emotionally damaging. My mother must have been quite devastated to discover she was pregnant again when I was only four months old. I can only imagine the senses my brother developed in utero based upon the facts that he was absolutely unwanted and the father was again questionable. There is only an eleven-month difference in our chronological ages. My mother must have been quite devastated to discover she was pregnant again when I was only four months old. As if that wasn't frightening enough, she soon discovered she was carrying twins! Imagine her emotional trauma as a mother who perhaps had not even overcome her postpartum stress and perhaps severe depression being impregnated again with less than desirable conditions. Apparently this pregnancy threw my mother into an emotional state that was insurmountable.

Her response to this trauma was a decision to try to abort the babies. On more than one occasion I'm told she intentionally threw herself down a flight of thirteen steps trying to precipitate a miscarriage. In June of 1948 my mother went into premature labor and delivered two male babies. The first baby died at birth and the second, my brother Douglas, was sent home from the hospital without much hope for survival. I'm told a Boy Scout troop built an incubator to be used at our home. My grandmother took responsibility for

Doug's care, and by the grace of God and her vigilance, his health situation progressed slowly. However, as Doug became a toddler and subsequently a young child he was noticeably mentally challenged. Surely if medical science had been as advanced as it is today Doug would have been diagnosed with fetal alcohol syndrome.

To make matters worse Doug's entire childhood consisted of his being considered less than, ill behaved, and not very intelligent. He certainly was given less attention than I was. His response to said treatment or lack thereof seemed to force him to do anything to be noticed even if it was negative in nature. He unfortunately spent a large part of his developmental years in my shadow. He certainly developed a severe inferiority complex that became deeply imbedded in his personality. The description that was generally placed on him was "he was bad." Usually the label my mother put on him when she was intoxicated was a "stupid son of a bitch." Obviously my parents were unable to do otherwise to eliminate the emotional damage that was being inflicted on him or that it would remain an issue for the balance of his life. Unfortunately Doug's response to repeated verbal abuse was acting out in negative behaviors that resulted in much more physical abuse from both my mother and father. When he was eight years old, he was struck by a car coming home from elementary school. The result of that accident was a severely broken leg that required a steel plate insertion in his thigh.

As my mother's absences became more frequent Doug's misbehaving became worse. At one point it became evident that his acting out was intentional because our mother would return home temporarily to have it appear that our family was not as broken and dysfunctional to juvenile court authorities who made home visits. Eventually Doug did have to be sent away from home for several weeks. When he came home he returned with some advanced knowledge of theft and street life skills that included obtaining and using marijuana.

Years later Doug was incarcerated for sexually abusing a young teenage male. He most probably had become a victim of that abuse himself while he was in jail. Anger became the only emotion my brother showed and it seemed to consume him to some degree for the balance of his life that ended tragically many years later. There were some offers from my mother's brothers to have Doug live with them but those times ended badly due to Doug's tendency toward disobedience, stealing, and self-destructive behavior.

Unfortunately, most family members eventually developed a total lack of trust in Doug and had little to no hope for a positive future. I still find that unsettling because no one really knew or acknowledged the physical and emotional abuse that Doug suffered constantly and professional help was never pursued. I was there and I know how severely he was punished because of his actions and belligerence.

As an adult he again spent many years incarcerated but did manage to marry and have a baby son. The marriage ended as a result of severe domestic abuse toward his wife. He was repeating the cycle of abuse he experienced in his childhood. Drug addiction to heroin led Doug to crime and even more punishment. He did manage to acquire a GED while in prison and began working on an associate degree. As is the case with ex-convicts, employment was limited and crime seemed more profitable.

Doug

REFLECTION

How unfortunate it is for young children who never receive God's greatest gift of love from their parents. The Word of God tells us the sins of the parents do not go unpunished and the results of said sin can be passed on to the third and fourth generations of children. These resulting sins are not always outward physical actions but also emotional abuse and neglect that present in many different aspects throughout one's adulthood. I present myself as a living witness that only the grace of God, delivered by the Holy Spirit and made possible through the blood of Jesus Christ, can reveal and heal wounded and broken spirits. That grace enables us to overcome the strongholds of victimization from our parents and grandparents. God gives believers victory over these generational sins and the effects they have on us and thereby proves the scripture that states, He that is within us (God and Holy Spirit) *is* greater than he (Satan) that is in the world. In contrast I consider my dear brother who did not choose to live an earthly life encompassed by God's love. I will share more later on how difficult it becomes to trust love of any sort when there was a terrible void from parental love. I dare say it becomes nearly impossible to trust a god that one does not see when there is little to no demonstration of love from parents who are given the responsibility and awesome opportunity to be examples of God's love. It also becomes difficult to trust the love that might be genuine from others we encounter in life. This hindrance forces one to question even the very existence of any capacity to give and receive love.

CHAPTER 6

On My Way

I graduated high school in 1965 with the highest of honors. Prior to graduation my guidance counselor informed me that I qualified for a college loan if I had someone in the family who was a homeowner and would sign for me. The only homeowner was an uncle who had inherited the family home of my grandfather. Imagine the excitement I experienced when I approached him to ask for his approval. His answer was an absolute "no" without any hesitation. Once again I had prayed to this "God" and my prayer was unanswered.

My senior year of high school and graduation was somewhat uneventful. My grandmother helped pay for my senior pictures because I was still receiving minimal pay for the houses I cleaned. Aunt Lella and Uncle Melvin bought me an absolutely beautiful yellow dress for graduation and shoes to match! I begged my father to come to the many award ceremonies I was a recipient in but he never once came. My mother was not living with us at the time and I didn't want her there anyway because she generally was such an embarrassment to me at that point.

Prior to the encounter with my uncle, several major corporations that visited my school interviewed me in April of 1965. They had been reacting to affirmative action laws recently passed. Their resolve was to approach suburban schools and interview high achieving minority students. Fortunately my counselor had the insight to recommend in my junior year that I add some commercial classes my senior year in case college would not be an option for me. During that one year I excelled in shorthand and typing as if a business curriculum had been my choice for years. The corporations quickly noticed my academic and business skills and scheduled me for additional interviews and testing. Much to my surprise the job offers that came were for an elevator operator and a mail clerk. AT&T presented with a much better offer and informed me they would hire me for a temporary position in July after my eighteenth birthday.

As promised I received my letter to begin working on August 2, 1965. It was a long commute from Oakmont to Pittsburgh and I had to be on a bus at 6:00 AM to get to work on time. Once again my dearest Aunt Lella and Uncle Melvin invited me to move in with them in the city and have a fifteen-minute commute on a streetcar to downtown. My original intentions were to move in with my fiancé's family since we had been engaged for a year. Once again what a total relief and blessing Aunt Lella and Uncle Melvin were during this life transition as they proceeded to force their way into where I was staying and took me to their apartment to live.

In May of 1966 invitations were sent out for a small house wedding in June. As was the custom, a shower was planned for me by my work associates. On Memorial Day of that year in the midst of a family gathering my fiancé invited me out in the hallway of the city housing apartment that I was living in with my aunt and uncle. Several other family members were inside enjoying the holiday. My fiancé proceeded to say, "I quit my job today!" When I asked him why he said, "My boss made me mad today and I told him f——u!" I could not believe what I was hearing given the fact that his father was retired and I would have been the only person working in a household of six people. That resembled the same poverty situation that I had grown up in. My response to him was, "You take this ring back and when you get another job we'll talk about marriage again!"

Before I could get the words out of my mouth he threw the ring that I had handed him out the window, balled up his fist and punched me in the face! Now as if the punch wasn't bad enough allow me to explain that my head was banged against a concrete wall so hard that my family heard the noise inside above the laughter and music that was going on. I immediately ran inside the apartment past my relatives and into the bedroom. I felt my face swelling like a balloon and I was seeing stars along with double vision. As my uncles and my father discovered what had happened they encouraged me to go back out and talk to my fiancé who wanted to apologize.

I thank God to this day that I stood my ground and absolutely refused to talk with him. Occasional knocking around of women was almost an accepted practice to my family but I knew even then that I wanted no part of that kind of lifestyle. I had seen my mother knocked around dozens of times and I swore I would never let anyone treat me like that. God himself gave me the discernment to realize if my fiancé was bold enough to attack me like that with my family a few feet away what would he do to me when they weren't around?

The result of the above situation was a cancelled bridal shower for which plans had been made as well as gifts purchased by my coworkers. Of course the small house wedding was cancelled and the immediate family notified. The embarrassment I endured from my coworkers was terrible for weeks. My mother actually said, "I can't believe you're can-celling a wedding just because he smacked you!" In the days and weeks following this incident I experienced stalking long before there might have been a name for that kind of behavior. My ex waited outside my work, rode the same streetcar, and followed me to the first floor doorway to my apartment building day after day. Needless to say, I was frightened and held on tight to some pepper spray. The positive result from this life experience was I began attending Central Baptist Church and registered at the University of Pittsburgh.

I'm so grateful that this particular turning point was in the direc-tion of the "God" that I recalled from my childhood. I also presumed at that time the hard time I had fallen upon was from the wrathful punishing God of my Baptist upbringing. Even though I had little to no concept of a loving forgiving God I still decided that turning to Him was the only thing I had left in my life after the devastations I had experienced by significant people who somehow didn't really love me at all. I was living with relatives, had lost what I thought was the love of my life, and still had horrifically low self-esteem. Thank God I found some semblance of redemption just by getting up and going to church on Sunday mornings. As with so many others I did experience one hour of uplifting moments and a snippet of hope for my future. At that particular time I had my little cousin Sharon who was nine years younger than myself who accompanied me to church and provided me a sense of helpfulness that she might not have to duplicate some of my mistakes. I registered for the winter semester at University of Pittsburgh to start in February 1967.

I'm certain my decision to totally remove myself from this relationship was considered a matter of good fortune fueled by complete fear of becoming a victim of domestic violence. Turning points from a certain instance can also be considered learning points. I knew even at age nineteen that my life was going to be totally in my hands and there was no one to blame for future mistakes but myself.

I continued to be stalked on many occasions but never considered getting back into that relationship. My aunt and uncle were seriously strict about my coming and going just about anywhere. Going clubbing was totally out of the question and the only opportunity to meet someone was limited by the very small number of black males in the office setting where I worked who were hired as mail deliverers, cleaning staff, or cafeteria workers. Even then I knew I wanted a more successful person as a significant other. I hadn't grown up in Waring Court where I was currently living and therefore was not invited to social events amongst other teenagers and young adults. I realize today that the restrictions placed upon me were undoubtedly the best thing for me as I had little to no experience with regard to dating and could have easily fallen prey to males who would have had a golden opportunity to take total advantage of me. My social circle consisted of my male cousins' friends who were younger than me. My cousins who were at that point my brothers never told me about the advances many of their friends wanted to make for an opportunity to date me. I took the absence of opportunity as more proof positive that I truly was a big ugly black bastard. Of course the few opportunities I had riding public transportation back and forth to work resulted in little to no attention that I noticed. Self-esteem was totally non-existent at that point in my life and I was totally consumed by guilt and shame from my teenage years.

CHAPTER 7

Real Love and Marriage

As I prepared to begin college with no thoughts of romance, it happened! I had called my beautician to make an appointment to get my hair done. Much to my surprise a man answered who told me he was taking calls and watching children for his sister while she did some chores. He continued by scheduling me for a late Saturday afternoon appointment. Unbeknownst to me this man liked my voice and decided to give me an appointment that he could be present for. After the call he proceeded to question his sister about me and was told I was a nice Christian girl. Hence, when I knocked on the door that evening, there he stood. Now I must explain that my appointment was to straighten my prewashed hair that resembled an afro long before they were in style! Thus my hair was absolutely wild all over my head and I had not a drop of makeup on. Ernie continued to talk to me as Janie did my hair and then suggested we go bowling later that evening.

We did go bowling as a foursome that evening and when Ernie walked me to the apartment door he gave me the sweetest kiss and asked me if I would like to go to church with him in the morning! Well of course you could have knocked me over with a feather but I said yes. The following Monday he called me at work and asked me out to dinner that evening. We had a wonderful dinner and as we prepared to leave the parking lot Ernie gave me a voluptuous kiss that nearly took my breath away! After that night Ernie met me at the bus stop every morning and took me downtown only after we had kissed ten or fifteen minutes on a side street across from the Civic Arena. We had to sneak to see each other because my aunt and uncle were very strict and found out that Ernie was separated for years but still married. He immediately filed for divorce a couple weeks after we met but I was not free to date him until he showed proof of the filing. In addition to that rule, one of my cousins had to accompany us wherever we went. Meanwhile, I was nineteen, Ernie was twenty-three and had a car. My Uncle Melvin considered a car a "rolling bedroom" of sorts so we had to have someone with us on all our dates.

We certainly found imaginative ways to have a few minutes together from time to time and immediately after his divorce was final he presented me with an engagement ring. It was five months after we had met. Today I must admit we were probably in lust rather than in love but we were married on July 8, 1967, at a small house wedding. We briefly considered a larger wedding but because of my previous engagement and marriage cancellation we decided against it. Also, neither of us wanted to have our alcoholic parents (my mom and his dad) to exhibit inappropriate behavior and embarrass us. We chose to use the money we both had saved to look for a house to buy rather than one evening of excessive food and drink.

Our wedding night was absolutely hilarious in that I was so nervous after the ceremony that Ernie's aunt and mother insisted I imbibe in a couple of drinks they had made for me. Well the last thing I remember that night was saying I was going upstairs for a few minutes but sat down at the top of the steps to rest. I woke up the next morning in bed still fully dressed and experiencing the pain of my corsage pin sticking me in my chest. Ernie was asleep next to me and had not bothered to try to wake me up (I think). Within a very few moments we heard a banging on the door and someone yelling. Much to my surprise, it was Ernie's elderly lady neighbor named Connie. She yelled, "Open this damn door so I can come in and clean up whatever mess is on this first floor." She continued by shouting, "Y'all continue whatever the hell you're doing." Needless to say I was totally embarrassed but Ernie let her in because he knew she would not stop yelling and arousing the neighbors in the row housing unit.

From that point on our marriage bliss continued and we celebrated our first year anniversary in our starter home. Needless to say the party we had ended with our relatives shouting and cursing in the street on which you normally could almost hear a pin drop it was so quiet. We were certainly on our way with our own home, two cars and both working with good jobs. The only thing missing was starting a family, which we had decided to do immediately after our marriage, but to no avail. We went on to experience many childless years of marriage. It finally occurred to us we might have a problem that money could not remedy. Once again I realized it might be necessary to make a plea to God as suggested by my grandmother. She bluntly told me I needed to get up on Sunday mornings and take myself to church. My excuse for not doing so was Sunday was the only day Ernie and I had a full day together without having to go off to work. At first I couldn't even imagine leaving our romantic Sunday mornings knowing also that Ernie would not be interested in doing so.

After quite some time we decided to have some tests done to see if we had physical problems related to infertility. Ernie tested fine and the doctor's resolve for me was to take fertility pills. The effects of those pills did result in several pregnancies none of which surpassed three months without miscarriage. While going to my gynecologist on a regular basis and taking the fertility drugs, it appeared I finally was pregnant past three months. Ernie and I were absolutely elated and I even started wearing maternity clothes that I had made. Imagine going for a monthly checkup and the doctor saying in a matter of fact voice, "You know, I don't think you're really pregnant!" I really thought I was going to have to be committed somewhere. I called Ernie on his job and told him he had to come get me immediately because I could not drive anywhere! The emotional trauma was devastating, to say the least. Medically speaking this was diagnosed as pseudocyesis or false pregnancy. In this experience a woman believes she is pregnant only to find that her symptoms of no menstruation, nausea, and abdominal swelling were not caused by pregnancy at all. Although exact causes are still unknown doctors suspect that psychological factors may trick the body into "thinking" that there is pregnancy.

I certainly had an intense desire in my mind and heart to be pregnant that was caused by my infertility and repeated miscarriages. I not only had a doctor who was treating me for pregnancy but I also had a swollen belly, enlarged sensitive breasts, and sensations I thought might be movement of the baby. The doctor apologized by saying I had an enlarged uterus and softened cervix. Obviously the positive urine test results that were relayed to me were absolutely *not* done because false pregnancy would always have a negative result. Upsetting doesn't begin to describe the psychological effect and embarrassment that I suffered and God bless Ernie who never did anything but be encouraging and understanding. In retrospect I believe Ernie was deeply affected by these mishaps himself but he never shared his innermost feelings in order to be supportive for my sake.

The next action that same doctor had was to continue to give me more fertility drugs. My fifth pregnancy was yet another miscarriage for which I was briefly hospitalized and returned very quickly to work in order to maintain my sanity and not sit around feeling sorry for myself. On the second day of said return, I began to have excruciating pain. There was no way I could hide the physical pain I was having even though I had learned to do so well in my childhood. I couldn't even stand in an attempt to make it to the restroom and hide. Once again I called Ernie at work and told him something was very wrong. His response was, "Oh, those pains are probably from your minor surgery related to the most recent miscarriage." However, even if I could be called inexperienced in this situation I knew there was something very different about this pain.

As I began to cry hysterically at my desk my boss told me the decision had been made to call an ambulance. One cannot even imagine the thoughts that were going through my mind as I considered the shame I would have to endure being carried out of a downtown office building in writhing pain and how quickly rumors would start. I immediately called my dear mother-in-law who lived perhaps ten minutes from my place of work and pleaded for her to come get me. I also did not want to be carried away from my desk on a gurney. I literally begged two male coworkers for help and they wheeled me in my office chair onto the elevator and down to the first floor of the building. Once we made it outside the building my mother-in-law as well as the ambulance were both there but I insisted upon going in her car to Magee Hospital.

The emergency room clientele immediately diagnosed the problem as an ectopic or tubal pregnancy. In explanation, a tubal pregnancy is when a fertilized egg stays in the fallopian tube and does not progress into the uterus as in a normal pregnancy. My fallopian tube had ruptured and treatment required immediate surgery to prevent dangerous hemorrhaging. The end diagnosis of this fifth pregnancy and recent surgery was I had been impregnated with twins in which one was a regular miscarriage and the other an ectopic pregnancy!

Those failed pregnancies took a terrible toll on our marriage even though Ernie never complained. On the other hand, I actually suggested we consider divorce because I obviously could not conceive and have the children he so decidedly wanted. After the ectopic pregnancy the company doctor who had to examine me before I could return to work recommended I go to an infertility specialist who, at the time, was quite renowned. As I reflect upon my emotional state I considered my entire life situation very dire. I had a very difficult time questioning why God would give me a taste of happiness and then snatch it away. I knew where those dismal thoughts would lead me. Because divorce seemed somewhat drastic, I decided to make one final attempt to reach out to the God of my limited understanding.

Touched

The next few chapters of this memoir describe the many instances in my life that *I know God touched me* personally. Those instances are quite numerous but necessary for me to share. I came to the realization in my life years ago that many occurrences in the lives of believers go far beyond coincidences in that there is no question God has intervened on our behalf. For that reason I chose to name those encounters "God-Instances." It is my prayer that as you read these God-Instances you will be encouraged to pray, meditate, and perhaps record similar circumstances in your life where you know without a doubt that God intervened and demonstrated His love and favor in your behalf. I call my summation of God-Instances a blessings list. Having these times written have blessed me countless times when I'm in the midst of troubles that Jesus himself told us we would have as believers. In John 16:33 Jesus told His disciples, "In this world you will have trouble. But take heart! I have overcome the world." When I read my blessings list I do indeed experience a peaceful assurance that "this, too, will pass." Certainly some might think as they continue to read, *really?* However, as you continue to read you will certainly see that my faith in God and the intensity of that relationship with Him is what is called today a no-brainer.

CHAPTER 8

Spiritual Growth and Change

I once again started attending church and did so on a regular basis. Subsequently Ernie began attending and joined Central Baptist Church in Pittsburgh. He was baptized and made a genuine commitment to serving God and Jesus Christ. That incident was a direct confirmation of God's word through Paul who told the Philippian jailor (and me) to believe in the Lord Jesus Christ and your whole household would be saved! For me, personally I needed to get to the end of myself and discard the belief I had that I could do life all by myself after surviving my hellish childhood. Today I know God heard my desperate cries and touched me in His own special way.

After I recovered somewhat from the trauma of those unsuccessful pregnancies, I did make an appointment to see the specialist my company nurse suggested. My first visit to the specialist was quite extensive but also encouraging. That doctor further explained that he had discovered cysts on my ovaries that inhibited formation of a healthy fetus so my body aborted them. The method of treatment was surgery, to put a wedge section in my ovary and remove the cysts; both of which would increase the possibility of fertilization.

Ernie and I continued to grow in and serve the Lord. Several months passed and we began investigating adoption through a church member who could be influential in our receiving a child. Meanwhile, the specialist recommended we plan an island vacation and stop trying so hard. There are certainly those reading this story who may have made intercourse a chore on the right day and hour as Ernie and I did and of course it's funny today, but it wasn't then! We both continued to pray and planned a trip to the Bahamas for the summer of 1972. In the meantime, I still agonized about being childless but also began to read and study God's word. On Mother's Day of 1972 I tearfully went forward for a special prayer and begged God for the opportunity to become a mother. I promised Him that if He blessed me with a child I would be the best mother I could possibly be.

Praise god! By the time Ernie and I began our trip to the Bahamas I was several weeks pregnant! Once the fourth month came and went we became hopeful. During the fifth month we both would constantly feel my belly for movement. By that time I permitted myself to become totally elated that it appeared we were finally going to have a child. I certainly was apprehensive when a baby shower was given for me by the same coworkers that had organized two bridal showers, but it was a magnificent event during my seventh month of pregnancy. There was still a part of me that had somewhat planned to never return to that workplace if the pregnancy was not successful. Ernie and I also received boundless love, prayers, and support from the Christians we had begun to fellowship with.

On February 8, 1973, Ernie went flying down the road so fast that a state policeman flagged us to pull over. Ernie abruptly told him I was in labor and literally left that patrolman in the dust! As Ernie prepared for and entered the delivery room He staggered to a point the staff immediately brought a chair and forced him to sit down. I heard someone say, "If this Franco Harris looking guy falls we'd have one hell of a time picking him up!" Finally the baby was delivered and Ernie literally hollered, "Nanc! It's a boy!"

I responded, "How do you know?"

Ernie screamed at the top of his loudest voice, "I can see his thing!" The whole room erupted in laughter as we shouted like little kids. After the baby arrived and I was being wheeled into recovery, Ernie looked at me with tears streaming down his face and said, "Thank you so much. I'll never ask you to go through that again."

My loving response was, "Don't say that, maybe we can try for a girl."

I'll never forget how wide-eyed Ernie got as he asked, "You mean you would go through that again?" to which we both laughed.

After being on pregnancy leave for eight months I had to make the decision as to whether I wanted to return to work. In one respect it seemed like a no-brainer because I didn't know any women of color that were stay-at-home moms, unless staying at home was their way of life anyway. After waiting so many years for a child I truly wanted to stay at home with him. However, my bosses continually reached out to me to return and continue what they labeled a career with the telephone company. What made the decision even harder was Ernie vehemently did not want me to return to work. I sought counsel with my pastor who wisely told me it wasn't always the quantity of time a mother spent with her children but rather the quality of said time. He went on to say there were mothers who stayed home with their children but resented it every day. I know today God spoke to me through that pastor according to His plan for my life. As I contemplated and prayed about this life event, I remembered a lady on our block that I passed every day on my way home from work, who obviously was a babysitter. I only knew her to speak to but I also could tell she was a very special lady. The children looked quite content and well taken care of as they would often be playing in her front yard waiting for their parents' arrival.

After praying I decided to attempt a visit with this kind lady, Mrs. Brown. That visit was the beginning of a Christian relationship that exists to this day. Mrs. Brown was assuredly a touch from God as I was blessed by her wisdom and direction to keep seeking God's will and that He would certainly answer. Ernie did not share the enthusiasm about a babysitter and told me if I wanted to live as comfortably as we had before our baby, he would gladly work two jobs. I'm grateful for the wisdom God gave me to inform Ernie that working two jobs would produce a negative result in his relationship with our son who we had named EJ. There were other issues pulling at me personally to return to work in that I hadn't ever developed trust in another person to provide for me. Neglect was an absolute dysfunctional result from my childhood and I wasn't interested in handing that responsibility to another (not even God!).

As the day approached for me to start back to work Ernie made life very difficult for me. On the Monday I returned to work my plan was to leave EJ at the sitter's and continue to downtown Pittsburgh. Ernie intentionally changed that plan and drove me all the way to the job. His action forced me to get out of the car and proceed across the street and into the building. That probably was the longest block I had ever walked and each step produced more and more tears. I couldn't even look behind to wave fearful I would change my mind and run back to my baby. The ensuing months were devastating at times as I tried to be a wife, a mother, and an employee with little to no help from Ernie. He held on to his intention to have me quit work and I insisted things were going just fine. I knew more than ever that I needed to return to studying God's word and believing Philippians 1:6 in which Paul tells believers, "Being confident of this, that he who began a good work in you will carry it on to completion until the day of Christ Jesus."

CHAPTER 9

New Beginnings and God's Favor

My yearning to continue studying God's word increased as my Christian sisters told me about Hardy Bible School where I could attend evening classes. I was elated as I began to tell Ernie I had found a way to continue studying God's word. I was in no way expecting his adamant negative response. By this time in our marriage I had become more and more independent which was in direct conflict with my well-meaning husband. My reaction to his comment that I could not go to a section of Pittsburgh at night provoked such rage in me that I stormed out of the house and proceeded to take a walk since EJ was already in bed and I hadn't grabbed my car keys.

As I stomped up the street a lady that I had seen on occasion stepped out of her doorway and spoke to me. I politely spoke back as she proceeded to ask me how I was doing. My nature was to respond, "Good, thanks, and you?" However, my immediate response was, "I'm walking at night like this because I'm angry at my husband and not ready to go back home."

She said, "Why don't you come and have a seat on my porch swing?" As I sat down Anne encouraged me to talk about why I was angry. I shared with her my disappointment about attending Bible study. She actually chuckled and asked if we could pray to which I hesitantly agreed because her chuckle seemed inappropriate.

As we continued our discussion Anne explained to me that she had been led by God for reasons unknown to go outside at which time I appeared. She went on to tell me she had been praying to God about leading a Bible study in her home that her husband would not give permission until some remodeling was done. Anne explained the reason for her chuckling was acknowledgement that perhaps God was working out His answers for both of us. She excused herself for a moment and returned with a brand new 1967 edition of the Scofield Reference Edition Bible that she informed me was a gift from God! We discussed the possibility of my having a Bible study in my home which was just a few doors from her house. Her specific advice was that I seek permission from my husband, even though I didn't much care if he didn't want it because he spent so much time in our basement on his ham radio after EJ was in bed. How could he possibly have objection to my entertaining some Christian women around our dining room table. Please be assured I consider this situation a God-incident and a phenomenal touch from God. It was the beginning of an amazing spiritual journey.

When I returned home I remembered Anne's specific instructions to lay hands on my Bible, pray, and ask God for a word. She assured me God would faithfully answer appropriately. I must admit I considered this a bit peculiar and my thoughts went to the possibility that I had gotten involved with a religious fanatic! Even so I followed her suggestion and opened my Bible. Well, much to my surprise the scripture was Ephesians 5:22 which reads, "Wives submit to your husbands as to the Lord!" I immediately slammed the Bible shut and reminded myself I had heard one needed to be careful following small portions of scripture without research. Today I know exactly where that thought came from. The enemy of our souls worked overtime to discourage me.

I approached Ernie with the intention to tell him rather than ask about the home Bible study. Much to my amazement he agreed and told me I should have coffee and something sweet to serve! As God would have it we began the weekly Bible study that grew so large Anne had to use my car to borrow folding chairs from a local funeral home! Many women, including myself, were blessed mightily as God used Anne to teach according to her gift. One of the subsequent blessings from this study was my being approached by a young man who was a coworker that observed me reading and study-ing my Bible at lunchtime. As we began studying and sharing other employees approached and joined us at our table. By God's favor and grace we were given permission to use various meeting rooms and employees from yet another downtown phone company facility joined us! I know today God was preparing me and building me up in His Word for my future in spite of the difficulties in my marriage that were occurring. We serve an awesome God and my praise will be continued until my very last breath.

In the midst of the blessings mentioned above, I was promoted several times on my job and given the opportunity to supervise employees. One major experience became a life changer for me. I was assigned the responsibility of supervising several female students from the inner city Fifth Avenue High School work-study program. To this very day I must say that task was the most challenging of my career. The girls had absolutely no work ethics and needed con-stant coaching as well as instructions for the task I had been assigned to complete. There seemed to be great resentment toward me and in some instances downright obstinacy to follow any directions I prayerfully and carefully gave them.

To this day I'm not certain why the company chose to have these girls assigned to me in the engineering department. One thing for certain, I had the greatest of understanding and compassion for these girls who undoubtedly had difficulties in their lives that they brought into their work experience. Being ever so grateful for the place from which God brought me my intention was to pay it forward with these girls to the best of my ability. On many occasions I had to rush into the restroom and into a stall to cry and pray because experiences with these young ladies pressed some buttons emotionally for me. I took their rudeness and insolence personally but refused to let them know how I was affected. In addition, I didn't want to give others in that work environment any impressions of failure on my part.

One girl, Karen, was particularly disrespectful and presented daily with a huge "chip on her shoulder" attitude. I became so annoyed one day I asked her to come down to the cafeteria with me so we could have a discussion. A meeting room would have been more appropriate but I honestly did not want to be alone with her because of her obvious rage. I cautiously told her that her behavior was totally unacceptable and if she disliked her work situation so adamantly she should leave and give some other young lady the opportunity. Her angry response was to call me an Oreo which meant black on the outside and white on the inside. I can't even begin to tell you how angry I became but that anger was a catalyst for me to share some of the details of my childhood abuse with this young lady. She was obviously astonished that I had those kind of experiences but had been able to rise above them to where I was in life at that present time. I ended that conversation assuring her she could do the same but if she chose not to, I would recommend her employment be terminated. Let me tell you, that young lady from forty years ago is still a beloved Christian friend!

Another awesome result of my experiences with Karen was a letter of recognition from the high school principal and the phone company coordinator of the work-study program. They were amazed at the total transition that had occurred in Karen. I recognized the favor God had bestowed on me and humbly wrote a response to the coordinator. As I prayed and prepared my letter, God reminded me of a passage where by faith Peter was able to heal a crippled beggar. Not that I'm comparing myself to Peter himself but rather the power God can give a believer. Peter told the beggar in Acts 3 verse 6, "Silver and gold I do not have, but what I give you is in the name of Jesus Christ." I had nothing of tangible worth to give Karen, but because of God's faithfulness and my fervent prayers, Karen and I both were blessed with what we needed. There's a song today that says in effect the world will say "it's all good" but there are those of us who know in instances such as this "it's all God."

Even more blessings ensued from the letters mentioned above. As God would have it, all the letters were forwarded to the director of the engineering department who subsequently shared them with his wife. His wife just "happened" to be a director of a school volunteer association for the city of Pittsburgh public schools. She requested my participation in the said program and I started tutoring at Martin Luther King Jr. school on the north side of Pittsburgh one morning a week. That effort expanded over time to a phone company organization that received extraordinary recognition by the city of Pittsburgh. This incident was again a touch and acknowledgement that "it's all God." Those elementary children I tutored became very special to me. God gave me the opportunity to bless children who were most certainly experiencing trauma in their very young lives. I always acknowledged their birthdays and Christmas and often gave them care boxes with personal items such as toiletries, washcloths, toothbrushes, toothpaste, deodorant, and hair supplies to teach them good hygiene so as not to be shamed by other students.

Chapter 10

Pregnant Again

Life and blessings continued as I grew stronger in the Lord. Lack of trust had always been an issue for me. I found it difficult to comprehend having trust in someone I could not see after being so grossly disappointed by my parents who supposedly had been designated to be trustworthy. I very slowly began to trust God with little things but still imagined I would be better served by trusting only myself for most things. It's incredible how patient God is with us as His kids! I can just picture Him standing in observation with His arms folded and perhaps sighing as He waits patiently for more trust from us. My biggest struggle was learning where to draw the line between being fiercely independent and yet a Christian woman giving honor, trust, and respect to my loving but controlling Christian husband. I even mistakenly began to think I could do just as well by myself.

In the midst of that marriage struggle I unexpectedly became pregnant! When I informed Ernie we immediately sought medical advice based on the hardships we had encountered before the successful birth of our son EJ. At the subsequent visit to our specialist doctor we were strongly advised to abort this pregnancy! There were multiple reasons for his suggestion in that there were cysts again on my one good ovary that in all likelihood would result in a natural abortion by the body sometime during the pregnancy. His opinion implied little possibility of a healthy baby and he felt it would be cruel and emotionally damaging to carry the fetus until perhaps the third trimester and then lose it. I was pre-diabetic and a smoker during the time of conception, both of which often result in a difficult pregnancy. He went on to say that if by chance the pregnancy went full term the baby could likely be deformed.

As I hysterically cried, Ernie asked the doctor what was the worst thing that could happen to me and if my life was in danger. The doctor assured Ernie my life was not in danger to which Ernie replied, "We'll take our chances." I, on the other hand, was so devastated and confused I gave no response.

I immediately began to fervently pray and ask God for His direction and protection. My lunchtime and home Bible studies continued as I grew spiritually. For weeks between the second and third trimester I was inundated with fear even as the prayers of my Christian friends and church members encouraged me to trust God. I began to pray without ceasing for a healthy baby. As the pregnancy advanced I asked God for a girl. One special occurrence happened with a little boy that I had been tutoring in the volunteer position during my pregnancy. For reasons unknown he became unresponsive and a bit belligerent. When I finally was able to prompt him to speak about his behavior he told me he was angry because I was pregnant! As we continued to talk I realized that in his limited life experiences pregnant was a bad thing. He hadn't known anyone who considered pregnancy a blessing. My heart absolutely ached as I explained that he and all children were a gift from God. As I shared this belief I experienced an even stronger desire to have my baby and share with him what an awesome thing the birth of a baby was meant to be.

At the beginning of my third trimester Ernie was stricken with severe back pain as he tried to ascend the stairs from our basement. From his screams I knew he was in excruciating pain. He begged me to call his mother because I could not help him upstairs by myself. When she arrived we together succeeded in pulling him up the one flight of steps but couldn't get him even close to the second flight to the bedroom. My dear mother-in-law insisted we call an ambulance and Ernie was transported to the hospital. His diagnosis was a herniated disc that subsequently led to surgery several months later. In addition, the discovery was made that Ernie had dangerously high blood pressure and further tests displayed damage to his heart muscle from a previous but unknown attack. Ernie was only thirty-three years old but obviously had the onset of heart disease that we later discovered was genetic.

Much later that same night Ernie was rushed to the hospital, I began to have severe pain as if I was having another miscarriage. Sure enough, I began to bleed and knew I had to get to the hospital. I called my sister-in-law who lived close by to come and get EJ as soon as possible. Next, I called Anne to come and take me to the hospital. As things evolved Ernie was in one hospital and I was in another. When Anne called me the next morning and asked me what she could bring from home my only request was my Scofield Bible she had given me, a notebook, and an ink pen or two. I knew without a doubt fervent prayer and specific intervention from God was necessary above all else. My immediate concern was to get back home to care for EJ and manage to visit Ernie. The diagnosis for my condition was a hole in my placenta most probably caused by my attempting to pull Ernie up the stairs. The doctor advised me what a dangerous situation this was in that if the placenta burst I would certainly lose the baby and perhaps I could fatally hemorrhage in as little as seventeen minutes. The hospital was a little further than seventeen minutes under the best circumstances and I absolutely refused to spend weeks in the hospital away from EJ, not even knowing how long Ernie would be hospitalized as well.

My decision was to go home with the promise that I would commit to being bedridden as much as possible until my baby could be taken by caesarian birth. God's answers to my prayers were immediate with the following blessings. Christian brothers and sisters gathered together and prepared two bushels of sealed meals that only needed to be dropped in hot water. Anne committed to stopping by the house at least once per day to do whatever was needed to be done. Our teenage evening babysitter chose to get EJ ready every morning to go to my daytime sitter's home and pick him up on her way home from school. My daytime sitter, Mrs. Brown, insisted upon keeping EJ from Monday to Friday totally out of Christian love as if I was still working! Certainly you understand my gratitude that God made a way out of no way through this family crisis. Even though there was absolutely no help available from my dysfunctional parents, Ernie's dear mom was poised to miss work and take care of all three of us as much as possible. She had long ago accepted me as her daughter and blessed me with a mother's love that I'm appreciative for to this day and the balance of my life.

As the pregnancy advanced well into the third trimester I continued to pray for a healthy baby and hopefully a girl. Then I boldly prayed for a pretty girl that resembled Ernie's family because I still had emotional scars and a deep-seated belief from constantly being called a big ugly black bastard. My original due date was August 27 but that day passed with a visit to the hospital with Braxton Hicks contractions or what's commonly known as a false alarm. My physician made plans to induce labor on September 14 but thankfully my beautiful daughter, Tonya, was born one day before, nearly three weeks after the original due date. It would be great to say this birth was a normal delivery but unfortunately it was a difficult one. A family friend who worked at the hospital and was somewhat overseeing the birth emerged from the delivery room to inform Ernie's family that there was a code blue emergency related to the birth.

Unfortunately Tonya was diagnosed with meconium aspiration syndrome that occurs when a newborn baby breathes a mixture of meconium (early feces) and amniotic fluid into the lungs prior to delivery. It's a serious condition because the airways are often blocked. (Information from MedlinePlus online). Most likely the "aging" of the placebo and the previously diagnosed hole in my placenta created the risk factors for this condition. In addition, very early before I knew about the pregnancy I smoked cigarettes. Both of these issues could have decreased oxygen while Tonya was in utero. Amen again! That is yet another magnificent touch from our awesome God directly to Tonya and me. I was made aware of God's answer to my prayers about my baby when WQED television asked permission to film Tonya for a documentary because she was such a gorgeous newborn!

CHAPTER 11

More Growth, Change, and Trials

My return to work was with little hesitation. Mrs. Brown was an incredible Christian woman who assured me watching EJ and Tonya would be a blessing with parents like Ernie and me. We moved to Monroeville in 1977 into a house that had three bedrooms and a huge backyard. Unfortunately Ernie's illness progressed prompting much abhorred absence from his job. It was not at all in his character not to be fully present as a father who made total provision for his family. His anger and resentment became nearly unbearable for me. Our move was further away from the Central Baptist church that we had been attending for several years and it became necessary to seek another church for fellowship and Christian growth. After visiting several others we joined the Garden City United Methodist Church that was nicely integrated and within walking distance to our home. I began seeking counseling at lunchtime and continued the Bible study once a week. One might have thought we had committed heresy leaving a Baptist church and joining a Methodist one with a Caucasian pastor no less!

Ernie and I both became active in our new church. Diversity was relatively new in this small community church. To some members combining races in worship was totally unacceptable at the time but others managed some acceptance. Pastor Gerald McCormick had a gift for drawing people to church fellowship and beyond. He began a relationship with Ernie while we were only frequent visitors. What we also found impressive was he visited Ernie during multiple hospital stays on a regular basis. Our children were also well received even though EJ had started attending private Christian school and didn't have the benefit of school buddies. We were somewhat shocked and disappointed when Pastor Gerald rotated to another church. The new pastor, David Keller, proved to be just as warm and genuine. He and Ernie began a bond that was exclusive to the both of them. I had attended an integrated school and had developed strong friendships regardless of color so the adjustment was much easier for me.

Ernie got totally involved in trying to encourage other people of color who lived in the immediate community to attend. Many of them did, but were not interested in becoming accustomed to traditional Methodist hymns. He made it his mission not only to speak to Pastor David but also to recruit a dear friend who sang at Hartwood Acres to direct the ensuing gospel choir. As Ernie was implementing his plan I began a search for an accompanist. When one was recommended the Lord made it possible for me to purchase a used piano for her home and we became an official choir. The music was certainly new to most of the original congregation but more people became accepting while others just stayed home when the newly formed gospel choir sang. In all fairness allow me to commend the Caucasian members who sang for the Lord and rejoiced in song right along with us from the very beginning. That racially combined choir became distinctive in our entire Western Pennsylvania district. I'll never forget the look on people's faces when Ernie showed up one Sunday singing with the chancel choir! His response to those who questioned him was, "If you folks can adjust to singing and hearing gospel I can do the same with traditional Methodist hymns." Allow me to say here, "What a man!"

As I continued to grow spiritually and attend small Bible study groups led by Pastor David my faith was greatly increased. We've all heard the saying "God is always on time." That was particularly true during that season of my life. God was certainly preparing me for life circumstances that would prove to be overwhelming. I was nominated for and accepted the position of lay leader in my United Methodist Church. In many instances that position was strengthening as I shared

God's love with other church members. Unfortunately I did a very good job covering up what was happening in my personal life. Pastor David and perhaps five others knew the distressing circumstances I was enduring. I had learned well from my awful childhood how to negate or totally hide emotional unrest. Unfortunately I began eating compulsively during those years. I have no problem admitting that divorce once again was a big consideration, not because I didn't love Ernie dearly, but his actions and reactions pushed emotional buttons in my wounded heart. Without the Lord and His Word delivered through Pastor David Keller my life would have been intolerable.

As Ernie's health problems increased, his depression became quite severe. His ego was drastically affected by experiencing constant pain and nearly uncontrollable blood pressure issues. Also, he determined it to be awful that I was working every day with absolutely no complaint about his inability to do so. All I wanted was for him to begin to take care of himself in order that he might live and continue to be the great father he had already evolved to be. Many times the only emotion he displayed on a regular basis was anger to me, the children, and his family because he was in constant pain. With his high moral standards of being a husband and father and not being able to fulfill these roles, he became emotionally overwhelmed. His heart had become only thirteen percent efficient and he was hospitalized at least monthly based on the swelling in his body from congestive heart failure. Many of his unacceptable thoughts and out of character behaviors were the results from lack of oxygen to his brain. His depression became quite severe and he became suicidal. He was out of control with compulsive eating even though he was extremely overweight. On occasion he actually got dressed and left the hospital to get food. I had to be sure to take his street clothes home with me each time he was admitted. He often would literally throw his hospital food trays against the wall and go to vending machines for food.

Thank God as things got worse my dear mother-in-love (not in-law) would come and take Ernie to her apartment for several days at a time to give me a break from my responsibilities as a mom, head of household, an employee, and a caregiver.

Allow me to share one incident that is humorous today but very stressful thirty years ago. I got up each morning, prepared the kids and drove them to Mrs. Brown's house where she would graciously feed them breakfast and see them onto their school bus. One morning, much to my surprise, my automatic transmission car would not start. I called off work and desperately thought about my options to do what I had to do every morning. Ernie's standard shift car was sitting in the garage but I had absolutely no clue how to drive it. With Ernie being a certified mechanic the only thing I ever had to do was get in the car and turn the key. I never even had to put gas in my car. I called my father (because it was early in the morning hopefully before the first drink) and asked him for instructions how to drive Ernie's car. My dad proceeded to tell me to imagine the letter "H" and described the different gears. That seemed easy enough to learn but then he told me about that horrible thing called a clutch and how one had to engage and disengage it all at the right time for shifting gears. I told the kids to stay in the house as I attempted to drive up to the end of our cul-de-sac and back home. I managed to do that within reason but I knew I needed more practice. I subsequently put the kids in the back seat of the car, loudly prayed in the name of Jesus and told them we would be okay as I practiced.

You need to know that in the housing plan where we lived you were always going up or down a hill. Need I say more? I can't even begin to tell you how many times that car was bucking and the kids and I were getting an education about whiplash. On one hill I really got stuck and tried for the kid's sake to pretend it was no big deal as the car drifted backward. Out of EJ's mouth came the question, "Mom, are you sure Jesus is watching over us?" I immediately answered yes, applied the emergency brake and initiated the flashers. Thank God a kind man stopped his car behind me, approached my car, and began slowly giving me instruction until I got a feel for the clutch. Might I say he was an angel sent by God! I choose to call it another big touch!

I didn't want to lose my nerve so I decided to do a trial run to Mrs. Brown's house. I could leave the car on her street (the level part of a dangerously steep hill even on foot) and catch a bus to downtown Pittsburgh. Thank God as I drove I got a little better. Praise be to God I made that eight-mile drive and then decided to stop at the hospital to visit Ernie because I had no intention driving any more that day once I made it back home. Ernie of course was surprised to see us in the middle of the day and knew immediately something was wrong. I suggested he look out the window and he saw his car. He literally held back his tears for the kid's sake because he felt so bad about not being there for us in such a crisis. I assured him we were and would be okay and of course, in his young innocence, EJ told Ernie how glad he was that Jesus took care of us on that hill!

CHAPTER 12

Testings

Marriage difficulties continued based on Ernie's health. The doctors again explained to me that because his heart was working so inefficiently, Ernie wasn't getting enough oxygen to his brain for rational thinking and behavior. They hesitated to put him on a transplant list until there were improvements in his weight. My utmost fear was he would follow through with his suicide threats that he made to me while I was trying to work. He had a gun collection that something needed to be done about. I was afraid to take the guns based on how angry I knew Ernie would get and perhaps have a heart attack arguing with me. I never knew what to expect when I came home from work so I would go into the bedroom first if he wasn't sitting up. His visits to his mom's apartment became less frequent because he couldn't negotiate the steps to the third floor of her apartment building.

I continued my counseling with a therapist as well as my pastor who both advised that I might want to consider having Ernie committed to a psychiatric hospital or leave our home with the children. Either of those options had the potential to have killed Ernie by suicide or heart attack and thus were totally unacceptable. I still hoped and prayed that God would intervene mightily. My church mentors at least insisted I remove the guns the first opportunity that presented itself. At that particular time I sought the Lord in the strongest spirit I knew. I was increasingly concerned about Ernie's safety based on his severe depression and suicidal thoughts. I learned many spouses who are chronically ill vent most of their anger and frequent rages on the people they love. I believed I could personally endure the rages that did not escalate to physical violence on myself. However, I became quite sensitive when our children began to notice drastic and negative behavior. I had to explain to them their dad's brain wasn't working correctly because his heart wasn't beating strong enough and they should try not to take his harsh words personally. My resolve right then was if the children demonstrated extreme emotional trauma, I would definitely take action because I knew the damaging effects that would result from such a level of dysfunction in a home.

On October 22, 1983, Ernie began a frightening outburst aimed directly at me as I sat down in the living room reading. By the time he reached the bottom of the six steps he bolted toward me and began hysterically punching me. I hollered and begged for him to stop with no response. However, when EJ stood at the top of the steps and screamed at the top of his lungs, Ernie stopped as if he had been in some kind of trance. Subsequently, I took the opportunity to run to the basement level of our home to try and quiet myself. Only once before did Ernie and I have a physical altercation at which time we exchanged one blow each. I assured him I would never be physically abused again. I had seen more than my share in my childhood and refused to subject my children to that emotionally damaging lifestyle. A few moments later, I heard Ernie's footsteps as he vehemently shouted he should blow my brains out. I pushed past him, grabbed my purse, keys, and Bible and off I went.

I must admit that I wasn't thinking as rationally as I could have been at that moment. Even as an adult far removed from domestic abuse, I often overreacted. I remember as an early twenties adult, crouching in a corner of our house listening to neighbors fighting in the house next door and praying Ernie would soon be arriving from work. I had no fear that Ernie would harm the children. Anyone who knew him knew what a devoted father he was who absolutely adored his two children we had struggled so hard to have. His whole purpose in life was to be a good father, perhaps to compensate for some shortcomings of his own father.

I chose not to call family or pastors because I didn't want them to push the issue of my having Ernie committed to a mental facility. I didn't doubt his love for me or the children. What I came to recognize was his devastating emotional pain—fearing he was destined to die shortly, and there was nothing he could do about it. My love for him and the strength that God gave me resulted in understanding that I would have never thought I'd have for anyone.

I went to a nearby Denny's and slowly ate and drank coffee for perhaps two hours until I got very sleepy and embarrassed. My decision was to remain in my car, which was parked under a streetlight and try to get some sleep. After resting but not sleeping, I chose to head toward work and got an hour or two of sleep in the employee lounge. I proceeded to my desk and began to work, not realizing fellow employees noticed my wearing yesterday's same clothes. After a few short minutes, my boss asked me into his office and surprised me by asking if I wanted to talk about the black eye and busted lip. Still because of shame and confusion, I didn't want to report it to the police as he suggested. He did, however, insist I go to a nearby hospital emergency facility to have my eye examined and perhaps stitches in my lip.

I complied and went to Magee Women's Hospital where they demanded I have the incident recorded and go to a shelter for emergency counseling. While I was there, I called my dear mother-in-love and explained what had happened the night before and I had been advised to stay a few days to try to reconcile over the phone with Ernie. My mother-in-love went immediately to the house, collected the children and their things, and off they went to Nana's, confused about what was happening. My mother-in-love had no fear about the children's safety, but did not want them to be subjected to the undoubted emotional trauma Ernie was experiencing after he realized what he had done. I kept in contact with my dear children who were most certainly confused but also sheltered from the seriousness of their father's mental condition. I lovingly explained to them that when people are ill and in a lot of pain, they often become irritable with people around them and they tend to say and do things they would not otherwise do. It didn't seem hard for EJ and Tonya to understand this explanation because they knew for sure their father loved them and me. I went further and asked them to think about some things perhaps they had said and done when they didn't feel well.

The second day at the shelter my dear pastor and two elders from the church visited and demanded I have Ernie committed to a place where he could be restricted and restrained from harming himself. I had shared with them the numerous times that Ernie would call me at work hysterically crying to inform me he was about to take his life with one of his many guns. In addition to his constant physical pain, he experienced overwhelming guilt and shame that he was incapable of providing for his family. Many mornings he would actually cry that I was leaving for work to support us rather than him. He felt he had been stripped of his manhood. These men's fears were certainly not unfounded, but in my spirit I was led to totally seek and trust God.

My love, compassion, and prayer led me to Psalms 37:3–5. There are several dates and personal circumstances that are scribbled all around this passage of scripture in my Scofield Bible. In this and subsequent times afterward, I desperately sought God's trustworthy and immediate direction. Allow me to paraphrase how the Lord spoke these words to me.

Nancy, *trust* in the Lord and do the good as you've learned from his Word.

Nancy, *delight* yourself in the Lord and He will give you the desires of your heart (even if you're confused; He knows your heart).

Nancy, *commit* your way to the Lord; seek His Word, trust in Him, and He will bring *it* to pass.

I made a decision to follow those words as I had done several times and listen to the still small voice that was in my spirit. I spoke to Ernie several times from the shelter as I'm sure his mother and sisters did, and we agreed that it would be safe for me to go home. The stipulation was the guns had to be removed from the house.

As I record this incident to share with you, I know without a doubt my decision to return home with the kids was an absolute touch from God. Living with Ernie was difficult to say the least but I suppose that was one of those instances believers speak about when Jesus carries us through tribulations. My commitment to continue based on the love I had deep down inside for Ernie was God given and I could not abandon him. Thank you, Jesus!

Our Family – December 1983

CHAPTER 13

Gone but Not Forgotten

Our family life circumstances continued with a little improvement especially over the 1983 Christmas holidays. Up to that particular point in my spiritual walk, I had never prayed and read God's word more consistently. No one can tell me to this day the previous incident wasn't a test of faith perhaps for both Ernie and me from the enemy of our souls. It certainly had the potential for all of our lives to have drastically changed. The physicians informed us Ernie's situation was very bleak and he would not likely be able to survive until a heart transplant could be performed. We almost had gotten into a rhythm when Ernie had to be taken to the hospital to drain fluid from his body as a result of congestive heart failure.

One evening, Ernie said he needed to speak to me about what he wanted for me and the children when he passed, which he had come to surmise was imminent. My response was absolute refusal to speak to my forty-year-old husband about his death. His mother, however, strongly encouraged me to listen to what Ernie obviously needed to say to me. Her exact words that I'll never forget were, "I'm his mother and if I was able to listen to my child that I gave birth to talk about his last wishes, you can listen as well." In the ensuing talk Ernie expressed his desires for our home, the kids' college education, and my future as someone else's wife. He expressed not expecting me to be alone for the rest of my life but would rather see me happy again. I told him, "If Jesus Christ himself would come and want me

I would only consider Him!" That was blasphemous for sure, but I very much resented having to talk about another husband at thirty-six years old when I believed mine would be healed. You've read the previous touches from God on my behalf and I believed with all my heart Ernie's healing would be another touch. I totally negated the fact that on two or three occasions God obviously answered no.

On March 15 Ernie waited patiently for his dear mom to come pick him up at the hospital. When they arrived home Ernie noticed that EJ had forgotten his lunch on the kitchen counter. It was a beautiful spring day and Ernie asked if he could drive his mom's car to the school and deliver EJ's lunch. Ernie's driving privileges had been denied the previous October based on lack of oxygen to his brain. Ernie was so happy his mom agreed to let him drive the six miles to EJ's school. After Ernie found and gave EJ his lunch he then asked his mom if he could drive out to his dear cousin's chicken farm in the country.

Unfortunately, Ernie never made it out to the chicken farm that day. He stopped at a red light and collapsed over the steering wheel. Ernie's mom began screaming for help and doing what she could until the ambulance arrived. The EMTs worked on Ernie all the way back to Forbes Regional Hospital where he was pronounced dead on arrival. By the time Ernie was brought to the hospital his three sisters were there and had been given the tragic news. My manager gently informed me that the hospital had called to inform me that Ernie's condition had changed and I should come as soon as possible. Offers were made to drive me but I agreed to use a cab, mostly so I could pray without interruption. Upon my arrival, my in-laws informed me that Ernie was gone. I immediately insisted on seeing him and actually began to shake him and pound hysterically on his chest as if I could revive him. I refused to believe he was really gone after so much prayer and anointing with oil.

Once I arrived home with my dear mother-in-love it wasn't long before Pastor David was at the door. His presence and prayer filled me with a very comforting spirit that I'm grateful for to this very day. When the children arrived home from school, Pastor David gently and lovingly informed them that their father had gone home to be with God. I'm quite certain I was still in shock because I don't remember how the children reacted. I suppose my gracious God blinded me of their pain as I struggled with my own. My dear mother-in-love had already made plans to stay with me and the children.

Long after we had gone to bed I absolutely could not sleep so I tried to slip out of bed without disturbing Ernie's mom. She did, however, awaken and ask me if I was okay. My response was, "I just needed to be alone with God for a while." I don't know why to this day I was afraid to go downstairs in the house, so the bathroom became my prayer closet. If there was ever a time I needed to hear from God directly, it was that night. As I had done so many times before, I pleaded with God to speak to me through His word, totally believing he surely would.

Much to my absolute shock and perhaps anger at the time, the scripture God gave me was Philippians 4:4-7. Even though I wanted to slam my Bible shut and hurl it on the floor, I slowly read and reread God's word to me that night? Verse 4 read, "Rejoice in the Lord always. I will say it again rejoice!" My thought was that God had disappointed me and I could not even imagine rejoicing about anything at that moment. Verse 5 says, "Let your gentleness be evident to all. The Lord is near." As far as I was concerned there was no gentleness in my thoughts and forbearance was totally out of the question. Verse 6 continued to read, "Do not be anxious about anything, but in every situation, by prayer and petition, with thanksgiving, present you request to God." My thought to that verse was, I had been praying for months, Ernie was gone and I was incredibly anxious. Finally, verse 7 was the only comforting portion of the entire passage because it stated, "and the peace of God which transcends all understanding will guard your hearts and your mind in Christ Jesus." I certainly wanted to believe all of those words but could not manage to do so for many years after Ernie's death.

I did have a great sense of gratitude that God had given me the courage and strength to stay with Ernie and keep our family together. I can only imagine what the outcome would have been for myself and the children if I had left him or committed him to a hospital during his last weeks. I don't intend to give the impression at all that it wasn't incredibly difficult day after day dealing with Ernie's mood swings for myself, the kids, and even the whole immediate family. However, I gratefully thank God for His wisdom and direction that I believe enabled all of us to love him until the very end.

Viewing Ernie's body in a casket was undoubtedly the hardest thing I had ever experienced. My first reaction was leaning down to give him a loving kiss. I had never loved anyone more than I loved him. It was also hard to stand with my children as they viewed their dad's body. At ages seven and eleven I'm sure they were quite confused even though they had been attending a Christian school and church all their lives. The Lord gave me a wise thought to share with the children. I told them that what they were looking at was like an empty candy wrapper and that the good stuff (meaning Ernie's soul) was with God!

Ernie had been active in two churches, was a volunteer fireman in the community where we lived, and an assistant to the midget football program. He was highly respected as a good Christian man who loved God and his family. The funeral home had standing room only every time we visited. It was quite impressive to watch a special ceremony the fire company had on Ernie's behalf. The church was totally packed into overflow seating at his funeral service. That gathering of well-wishers started as a funeral but concluded as a celebration of one of God's children going home long before "celebration" of a deceased person was customary. As we traveled to the cemetery I happened to look back at the procession of cars. I had to have the children then look back to recognize the vast number of cars behind us as far as we could see for at least a mile. That certainly spoke to them about what others thought of their father.

Needless to say, the following weeks were unbearable. I couldn't imagine how I would ever be able to live and rear my children by myself. Even though I was totally surrounded by family, church members, and friends I was emotionally devastated. Unfortunately, once again my thoughts were driven to contemplating suicide. I actually made the decision to commit suicide but took time to decide which way I would carry it out so EJ and Tonya would not have to find me by themselves. One afternoon as they were outside playing, I locked the doors. My logic was they would have to get an adult who had a key to come in the house with them.

To this day I cannot explain the strong tendencies toward suicide that I experienced in extremely traumatic situations. Much later I will briefly discuss these tendencies that are so strong and unfortunately numerous in adults who had adverse childhood experiences (known as ACE). My only thoughts in regard to my children were they would be better off without me, and Ernie's loving close-knit family would surely step up and raise them better than I thought I ever could because I had no good family life to draw examples from.

Get ready for another miraculous touch from God! As I lay on the bed prepared to take the prescribed sleeping pills, there was a knock on my door. Of course I had no intention in answering. Suddenly, my dearest friend Dawn, who was more like a sister, was in my house and headed up to the bedroom. My first reaction was anger that she had somehow gotten into my locked house without a key! Needless to say, she found me hysterically crying as she held and rocked me as if I was a little girl. Once again God saved me from self-destruction and my children from becoming orphans. He used Dawn in a mighty way and we both realized with amazement how faithful and personal He can be to us.

After a while Dawn went next door to my dear friend Gerry's house to ask for her help. I had previously started remodeling and changing things in the house because everything reminded me of Ernie. Unfortunately, I didn't have the presence of mind to do one room at a time. Gerry, her husband, Moo, and her family had become the greatest of friends over the six years we had been neighbors. Before I knew it there were several women in the house trying to fix the terrible mess I had made.

After that incident I knew I had to involve myself with something to look forward to. Ernie and I had often talked about taking the children to Disneyland so I began planning that trip. Gerry began watching the kids off to and after school to save me from having to travel to and from Mrs. Brown's house several miles away each day. At that point she was Aunt Gerry and her husband became

Uncle Moo. They happened to have been Caucasian but that was of no consequence to any of us. We all loved each other dearly. Uncle Moo and Ernie had become like brothers. Moo had older daughters and took it upon himself after Ernie's passing to be somewhat of a surrogate father to EJ. In addition, Dawn's husband, Dennis, was also like the brother Ernie never had. They loved and supported me and the children in numerous ways for years.

CHAPTER 14

Wild and Destructive

At age thirty-seven I began to act like the single young adult I had never had the opportunity to become. I married at age twenty and had absolutely no experience being a single adult. Even my mother-in-law strongly encouraged me to take some time for myself. As I began to feel comfortable leaving my children at home or with Dennis and Dawn, I began frequenting singles bars and clubs on the weekends. Needless to say, my church attendance went down and I developed some destructive habits.

In the midst of my party hardy attitude, I met a man at a birthday party that was an absolute charmer. He was tall, handsome, a great dancer, and fun to be with. Even though it had been quite some time after Ernie's passing, it was less than two years and I felt guilty about this new friendship and began to sneak to see him at his place while the kids were occupied with other things such as movies, bowling, or skating. Unfortunately, after a few months I realized my friend had a problem with alcohol. Don't get me wrong, I drank right along with him for years until it became frightening. Based on the fact that my mother was an alcoholic, I had fears of becoming one myself. I also experimented with marijuana for the first time in my life at age thirty-eight!

My mother's alcoholism progressed to the point that I started to seek help for myself from a group called Al-Anon that met during lunchtime at a church across the street from my work. My participation in that group forced me to take another look at what I was doing with alcohol. From that group I also recognized I was unknowingly exhibiting some patterns of children of alcoholics! Imagine how shocking that was to see myself becoming caught in a cycle that would surely lead to more self-destruction. It took me a while to make the comparison because I was in no way abusive to my children. If anything, I overcompensated for their father's death in addition to my guilt and shame for things I was doing.

Thank God my involvement in Al-Anon for people who deal with alcoholics led me to another twelve-step program called ACOA that represents Adult Children of Alcoholics. What a rude awakening this program proved to be. I had previous problems with compulsive overeating and had been attending Overeaters Anonymous for years. However, what I didn't realize was I had transferred my addictive tendency from food to alcohol! I totally believe that even though I certainly strayed during those years God's grace was extended to me. I had always known there was something quite different about my actions and reactions to life situations, but attendance at these groups was quite a revelation to me and it wasn't pleasant. As I went to meetings and weekend retreats, I was forced to get honest with myself. I started attending Alcoholics Anonymous in addition to the other twelve-step programs. It was encouraging to recognize the natural progression from said groups was a closer relationship with a higher power that I chose to call God. This newfound knowledge was not a coincidence but certainly a God-incidence as well as another mighty touch from God.

Of course, I had to end my relationship with my friend who was not interested in recovery, as I had stopped drinking alcohol. I continued my journey of recovery and established friendships that still exist to this day. It was such a blessing to be open enough to admit my character defects and begin to trust God to remove them. However, after several years of recovery I managed to slip into a relationship with a highly respected member of Alcoholics Anonymous who just happened to be married! Yes, my whole truth must be revealed to maintain my healing journey and perhaps for someone else to heal as a result of my total honesty. Even though we both knew our affair was wrong, we blindly continued.

After two years that married man moved into my home with my total permission under my presumption that we were totally and completely in love, which was true on my part. I knew deep inside that it was wrong in God's eyes. When someone would make mention of our living together I would laugh and say we were "practicing marriage." Someone who loved me very much asked me how was it I trusted this man not to eventually do what he was doing to his wife to me. Of course I ignored that thoughtful suggestion and continued deeper into the relationship. That situation caused me much stress and what seemed like insurmountable guilt and shame.

We actually had the nerve to attend his very large church but to sit in different sections rather than together. One day, as the service was ending, I saw the woman I recognized as his wife approaching me. I immediately jumped up and headed in the opposite direction and out an exit door. I was stunningly dressed in a silver fox mink coat and heels. Imagine my surprise when I discovered the only way to escape was up a muddy hillside! Now imagine how foolish I realized the whole situation had become. Luckily I made it up the hill and to the place where we had parked the car without being "caught" so to speak.

I believe even today that this man loved me as much as I loved him but was enticed to sneak off one Saturday all day and evening with another woman. I could easily assume he was with another woman because he ignored my many calls to his cell phone. Also, I put on my investigator hat and called his job, which is where he told me he would be. Obviously he was not and had not been on the job that day. When he finally managed to return home at a time approaching midnight, I immediately informed him he needed to pack his things and get out of my house. Need I say it was with much profanity that I had never used. I went on to tell him that if his things were not gone that next day they would be at the curb Sunday night for garbage collection.

REFLECTION

Allow me to begin now to share what I understand as chastisement from God that is spoken about in Hebrews 12:11. That passage paraphrased strongly suggests that chastening at the time it is happening can be devastating. Nevertheless, afterward we as believers are blessed by God himself and given more righteousness as we experience that chastisement. I've come to imagine my spiritual self as a house with many rooms that needed cleaning in varying degrees. Thanks be to God that He accepts us just as we are when we commit to serving Him through the sacrifice of Jesus Christ. God then lovingly proceeds to cleanse those rooms (or issues) that would hinder us in our Christian walk toward maturity in our soul, spirit, and body. The word perfect is often used to describe our goal as Christians but we also know that sinless perfection is not attainable in this life. In Philippians 3 we are encouraged by Paul to forget those things in our pasts that resulted in wounded emotions and look forward to God's healing according to our level of faith and trust in Him. As I've moved from the milk of the word to solid food and now the meat of His word, I agree with Joyce Meyers who says, "New level; more devil," but thankfully I know God will strengthen me and keep me through all my life struggles!

CHAPTER 15

To Teach Me to Trust

Ten years after Ernie's death in 1984 and my self-destructive behaviors, there was a part of me that felt I had finally arrived. I had my great job, EJ was in college, and Tonya was on her way. Their college education was a promise Ernie and I insisted upon. I remember I was anxious for years how I would be able to send them both to college. Today I certainly recognize my total financial provision for their further education was an unrealistic expectation. I'm grateful for the partial scholarships, their willingness to participate in work-study, and my help as much as possible. God certainly made a way in that their college education was yet another example of His touch in spite of my constant worry and lack of trust in Him to provide. It had been ten years of God's provision and blessings in spite of my wayward behaviors. Perhaps I was beginning little by little to discard even more of my childhood thoughts of a wrathful punishing God even though to some extent I believed I deserved some. I suppose the immense guilt and shame I experienced constantly during those years was sufficient punishment.

I realize today that trusting God was a huge area in my spiritual house and I was only willing to give Him a very little bit in a few rooms at a time. On April 1, 1994, I was rear-ended on my way to work and suffered severe whiplash that I sought immediate treatment for. I refused to take off from work in spite of excruciating pain. My early childhood physical abuse had left me with a very high tolerance

FROM TOUCHED TO EXALTED

level for pain as well as an uncanny ability to cover it up or ignore it. Our department had undergone some serious downsizing and I felt responsible to carry my share of the greatly increased workload. It just so happened the driver of the vehicle was a city of Pittsburgh policeman and even though I consulted a lawyer the case never went anywhere.

In addition to the results of the car accident, stress from my job became quite intense. After almost a lifetime of extremely stressful situations my physical health became an increasing problem. I continued with physical therapy on my lunches but the condition worsened. I extended my work hours to compensate for the thirty-minute or more breaks I took twice a day. My mobility decreased to the point it was extremely difficult to even make it to the restroom. I can't begin to count the times I would slip into the nearby stairwell to pray and cry.

I began to see an orthopedic specialist who informed me I had degenerative joint disease specifically in my knees and my spine. The knee problem was a result of my being overweight for years as well as genetic. The cervical portion of my spine was affected by a back surgery at the age of eighteen months that upon my investigative request medical records made mention of polio. I do vaguely remember having to wear special shoes with braces. Unfortunately, my mother's reflection changed constantly in regard to this surgery that at the time extended down my entire back. When I sought a response from other family members about this medical issue they had no information to offer probably because my mother's account changed so many times. The extra pounds in adulthood contributed to lower back pain. Yet another diagnosis for my pain was fibromyalgia.

By June of 1994, it became impossible for me to continue to work after using up four weeks of vacation days trying not to call off sick. I continued to seek treatment and was hospitalized based on the difficulty I had walking. As time progressed and I went from doctor to doctor and through pain management therapy, it became more unlikely that I would be able to return to work just six months short of thirty years of service for full retirement benefits. The mere thought of not working resulted in a bout of depression and I again contemplated suicide.

I was actually in St. Francis Hospital's psychiatric unit trying to open a window to jump out. My mental capacity was certainly depleted to think that after the initial search at admission for any object that could be used to hurt myself I would be placed in a room that the window would open. My logic was I would be a useless human being without a job and would end my life on welfare as my immediate family members had been doing for years. When I realized I couldn't jump, I made plans to drive off a hill once I was released from the hospital and defiantly told a nurse of those intentions. The nurse's response was indeed another touch from God when she informed me that if I committed suicide that tragedy would be the legacy I'd be leaving for my children. She went on to tell me that a very high percentage of children repeat the pattern of suicide based on their parent's choice. Even though I had no regard for my own life I had not thought about the total effect my death would have on my adult children. I asked a dear friend to bring me a cassette Bible study by T.D. Jakes that I listened to every opportunity I could when I wasn't in group therapy. I distinctly remember feeling all alone and helpless with no one to love and help me much less trust him or her to take care of me. That mindset totally negated the possibility that God would take care of me.

In June of 1995 I was threatened with dismissal. Against medical advice I attempted to return to work. My local managers encouraged me to come and just show up and not be concerned about work performance for six months until I had thirty years for retirement. The demand for dismissal was from corporate headquarters whose only concern was more downsizing. I dressed and made it to the corner bus stop because I did not trust myself to drive. As God would have it a neighbor who also worked for the same employer stopped and offered me a ride. She knew about my situation and informed me she would give me a ride daily to work. I made it through two days when I realized I simply could not continue. I had a change of clothes and bathroom accessories in case I couldn't make it to the restroom. I was subsequently dismissed and began living off my retirement fund. I applied for disability from my employer and painfully endured many doctor visits that confirmed the severity of my medical condition. Even after all medical reports were submitted, I was formally denied.

It would be nice to be able to say that at that point I was willing to trust God for my well-being but I absolutely was not. I continued to fervently pray but kept my devastating circumstances personal. I found myself bombarded with guilt and shame from being unemployed, but not suicidal. I was lovingly encouraged by a dear friend to apply for social security. My concept of social security was yet another handout but in desperation I called and scheduled an appointment. By the time I showed up for the appointment, the representative had already reviewed my work history and extensive medical history. I proceeded to inform her that I was in the process of seeking legal counsel. I had been praying according to scripture for God's favor and once again he touched me. The representative explained to me that what I would receive from social security was my money that I had accumulated over those decades and I was entitled to it! She also strongly advised there was no need for legal counsel and approval was nearly a certainty without it. Once again thanks be to God my case actually was approved.

Today as I reflect upon this situation, I am totally convinced that God permitted this life circumstance to teach me how personal and faithful He is. It was chastisement for sure but was also a lesson that became a blessing in regard to trusting Him. I've come to believe there are three dynamics we experience regarding God's will. There is His "perfect will" that we can only experience in different seasons of our lives but it is often short lived based on our sinful nature. God's "permissive will" also plays a significant part in our spiritual growth in that He permits certain occurrences so we might experience His grace and mercy as He delivers us from them. I compare this concept to a parent who has forewarned a child time and time again not to touch something hot. Eventually the parent might decide to stand close by and allow the child to slightly touch the object and quickly snatch the child's hand away. Finally, there exists a spiritual bankruptcy where we find ourselves "totally out of God's will" but His unconditional love once again triumphs as we attempt to repent and seek Him.

Again I must say I still was anxious with two children in college at the same time. Social security would not be sufficient to meet my financial obligations. Now just let me tell you once more about the God we serve (if we so choose)! Two years after the onset of my chronic illness and second request, I was granted a disability pension from my employer. I was totally baffled as to why the initial request was denied and questioned why. The response was it was part of their established procedure.

My difficulty in trusting God was certainly waning after all He had done but I still couldn't imagine doing anything more than existing with the drastic reduction of my income. Apparently I hadn't gotten to the end of myself and what I determined was still mine to do alone. I began sewing in very small increments of time for distraction from my constant pain and to achieve a sense of accomplishment in my daily life. I insisted on having purpose to my life. As I continued the result was even more bad health as I ignored my pain. There was never enough financial gain to call my sewing venture a job or even a lucrative hobby, but the love and fellowship I experienced with other friends, acquaintances, and family was a blessing in itself. I had learned the devastating consequences of pain that resulted in depression but suicide was no longer an option. The good news is, I began to seek even more of God as I realized my health continued deteriorating. All I wanted in this life was assurance that my children completed their college education and began successful careers.

CHAPTER 16

God's Healing Touch

In early 2002 I discovered a lump in my right breast that I hesitantly knew I needed to get a mammogram hoping it was just a cyst.
When I went to receive said mammogram and further digital testing,
I was diagnosed with breast cancer! I was shocked at the urgency
the technicians expressed as they arranged for me to see a surgeon
immediately. Just prior to the above testing, I had been blessed by a
member of my church family to change my primary care physician.
Immediately after the testing results I made an appointment with my
new physician whom I had trusted from the very first visit perhaps six
months prior. She was vehemently angry that she had not been consulted and was totally against the surgeon my case had been assigned
to. She at once made a call to another surgeon and arranged for me
to see him that very day! Only God knew exactly what I needed and
prompted my friend to have me change physicians at what became a
critical health situation. Allow me to say, "You go, God!"

There are no words to express my gratitude to my sister-in-law,
Janie, who stepped right in and accompanied me to appointment
after appointment just as her brother Ernie or then deceased mother
would have done. I long ago stopped thinking of her as a sister-in-
law and chose to consider her a sister-in-love even to this very day.
We were rushed to a total of three doctors in one day until we sat
together in the oncologist's office. Janie listened and took notes as
the doctor informed us that I was in a dangerous stage four breast

cancer situation that needed immediate chemotherapy to reduce the tumors before he could even consider performing surgery. That was the beginning of a very long healing journey.

I certainly acknowledged the seriousness of my situation but my very first question to the doctor was whether I would be able to go on a cruise with my daughter that I had been paying installments on for a year! His response was a disappointing no that I somewhat ignored. My reason for not accepting his answer was I had a grandmother who was diagnosed with breast cancer at age seventy-nine, endured a total mastectomy as well as radiation and continued to live until nearly age ninety-four! I concluded that she served the same God that I did and He was able to anoint me with that same kind of healing. Finally I was trusting God to the fullest degree in this circumstance.

At my first chemotherapy session the Lord placed a ninety-some-year-old lady in the chair next to me. As we began to talk to one another she told me she had plans to go shopping at a department store on a bus after her treatment! She went on to tell me that I wouldn't begin to feel sick and nauseous until the second or third day after treatment. I shared with her my desire to go on my paid cruise and she saw no reason why I shouldn't plan to go. At my postchemo treatment I was still seeking the doctor's permission about the cruise and his response was still no. However, as I was leaving the office a nurse encouraged me to do what I *felt* like doing. She went on to say that I would be right in the middle of a round of chemotherapy and the last week would be when I'd start feeling really weak and exhausted. I thought to myself, "Just look at God confirming His answer to my prayer about the cruise!"

Tonya's degree was in music therapy that included training to assist physically challenged patients. Let me tell you, she totally took over my care during the cruise that included a motorized cart, provision for embarking and disembarking the ship, and special sightseeing tours that could accommodate the cart. Furthermore, she had sprained her ankle a few days before the cruise and was on crutches! We had a wonderful time on the cruise even when I had a drink or two and nearly ran her and some other passengers over with my cart on the elevator. She teases me to this day about that incident.

Another great happening on the cruise was acceptance of my baldness. Janie had insisted I get a wig immediately after my first chemo even though my hair had not started to disappear. However, by the time I went on the cruise my hair was totally gone and it was too hot for a wig so I wore straw hats constantly until a woman asked me why I was doing so. I showed her my bald head and she asked me hadn't I noticed several young women intentionally sporting their bald heads and how beautiful they looked. After that, I boldly presented myself without anything on my baldy head even after I came home! I actually took a picture with two bald gentlemen in my church family and totally ignored the stares I received from strangers in other places.

Nancy – Bald with Hat   Nancy – Bald with Pasquale and Tom

My second visit to the oncologist was an anointed experience. He literally closed his eyes and gently touched the area of my tumors. He opened his eyes with a look of absolute amazement and said, "Your tumors have drastically reduced in size." My immediate response was to shout at the very top of my voice, "Thank you, Jesus." That outburst was certainly not what he expected as his face turned bright red! I think perhaps my sister-in-love, Janie, was a bit embarrassed but we both began to weep tears of gratitude as we acknowledged God's healing grace.

As I continued chemo treatments God completely supplied every one of my needs through Janie and my dear friend Dawn. In

September the oncologist informed us that the tumors had reduced to such a degree I might only need a lumpectomy rather than mastectomy. However, postsurgery I was informed a total mastectomy had been required based on the aggressive nature of the cancer cells that had also metastasized into the lymph nodes in my right arm, so the majority of them had to also be removed. God sent an angel in the presence of a nurse, Maria, from my church family whom I barely knew that spent the night of my surgery at my bedside. In the morning she lovingly washed and cared for me with her assurance that God would indeed see me through this tribulation. We are devoted friends today who encourage each other in our spiritual walks.

After my mastectomy I had devices that needed drained and cleaned daily. I dreaded the very thought of this task as I grieved the total loss of a breast but once again God stepped in. Dawn came every day after her work to do whatever I needed including emptying those drainage devices and making sure I ate! On one occasion God sent a young lady whom I had sewn for, to visit. She proceeded to administer the drainage even though I was embarrassed to have someone I didn't know well to be doing something so private to what I felt was a deformed body.

At my postoperative visit my oncologist informed me I needed four months of additional chemotherapy and extensive radiation afterward based on the pathology report. Unfortunately, after the third chemo treatment my immune system had been so diminished I developed a horrible infection surrounding my surgery scar. Emergency surgery was required that entailed a blood transfusion based on the levels of poison in my blood. I could sense how drastic the situation was as I observed my surgeon's face. Today, I surmise he and the oncologist had little expectancy of my surviving this complication. Once again total praise to my God who sent His extraordinary healing touch. Months after my surgery and radiation, my well renowned surgeon requested me to speak at the Hillman Cancer Center in Pittsburgh. He graciously introduced me as his miracle patient! I was blessed to be able to share my testimony about fourteen consecutive months of treatment with women and their families to give them hope.

Upon completion of the treatment, knowing the first five years were extremely critical, I thanked God that He had saved my life thus far. I knew I had received His love throughout the cancer ordeal from Janie, Dawn, my church family, and countless others. I acknowledged that through these wonderful people I personally experienced God's agape love. Needless to say, I became closer and closer to God. I knew personally that a huge transition takes place when one has been close to death. Each day was a blessing that I no longer took for granted. My prayer, meditation, and study of God's word became extensive and more fulfilling to my spirit and soul.

At that particular point in my life I acknowledged God's faithfulness throughout my life and had only one request. I wanted to enjoy the experiences of having a grandchild. My daughter was married but not planning pregnancy at the time. As God would have it, a niece in the family gave birth to a beautiful baby girl in July of 2003. She needed a sitter on Wednesday of each week and was gracious enough to allow me to provide that care. From week to week keeping little Senea literally gave me purpose that I much needed for those few hours. I would hold and rock her for hours and when it was time to nap, I made a pallet on the floor and we slept together. We became bonded in God's love through each other and remain so to this day.

In answer to my request, God blessed me with my first grandchild, Cameron, on July 11, 2005! She was absolutely gorgeous like her mom Tonya. The love one receives from a grandchild is indescribable. I was able to spend countless hours with her the first two months of her life. As I did so I noticed my attitude about continuing to live began to change. Looking forward to completing five years cancer free became much more important to me. I subsequently decided to plan a celebration of my sixtieth birthday and completion of five years in remission. That glorious event took place on July 21, 2007, with over 150 attendees to whom I will be eternally grateful for their sharing of that special occasion with me.

CHAPTER 17

Damaged Emotions

Long before I knew it existed, stress was a daily component of my life. Even the times when things seemed somewhat normal on any given day the residue of previous stressful days remained in my young body. I recall having physical problems with constipation that was probably the beginning of chronic irritable bowel syndrome. My grandmother recognized the problem and a dose of ex-lax laxative became a weekly occurrence. I wonder today if she had similar problems because that laxative was always on top of her dresser. The unending stress was taking a physical as well as mental toll on me. The unquestionable result of this never-ending stress from abuse was damaged emotions.

I recognize today that a rash I had on my arm at age ten was diagnosed as impetigo. I'm certain it was a direct result of my mother literally throwing my grandmother out of the house one dark cold night during one of her drunken rages. That skin disease got markedly worse but my parents ignored it by making the assumption it was the result of bed bug bites that I needed to stop scratching. My grandmother was afraid to intercede even though she no longer lived with us. Once again, my Aunt Lella stepped in and took me to visit with her and her family. She immediately took me to Children's Hospital where I received much needed treatment. I have no idea if the medical professionals informed my aunt that the medical diagnosis might have been stress related.

Many people have little to no understanding how damaged one can become emotionally. Yes, we see those who act out on their wounded emotions with violence toward themselves and others. They are the ones that are noticed and often given either hatred or compassion. It's difficult for people who haven't had to live with damaged emotions to even begin to relate to how deeply imbedded the hurt becomes. After many years of group and personal therapy, I was forced to acknowledge my inner child.

> How many times . . . have you
> encountered the saying, 'When the student is
> ready, the Master speaks?' Do you know why
> that is true? The door opens *inward*. The Master
> is everywhere, but the student has to open
> his mind to hear the Masters Voice.
> —Robert Anton Wilson,
> Masks of the Illuminati

How pitiful that there are certainly millions of people who have deep-seated emotional issues that are suppressed or repressed as they struggle to display some form of normalcy. I can say for myself personally I knew my emotions were very different from other people as I watched their actions and reactions even to daily life events. I recognized the wounded little girl inside me that dominated my thoughts and actions even as an adult. What some people considered my being nice all the time was actually my trying to be the good little girl from my childhood who wanted so desperately to be loved and accepted. Today, I know that behavior describes codependency. What I failed to realize as an adult was that codependency fueled some very *not okay* feelings as I experienced emotional pain once again when others grossly disappointed me and failed my unrealistic expectations. My being nice to others was extremely genuine but sometimes to a fault based on my own emotional needs. I sadly recognized the fact that I had dire emotional needs, and then denied them in order not to feel the pain.

I don't know the technical ins and outs of how devastating emotional wounds affect our physical health and mental well-being but what I know for sure is I experienced the hurts from my childhood well into decades of my adult years. Even the salvation of my soul through Jesus Christ only began to invalidate my negative thoughts I struggled with on a daily basis. We wounded kids learn very well to wear masks of deception that hide our true feelings. I'm certain all individuals have or have had struggles with feelings to some extent, but to those who have suffered abuse and neglect that struggle is much greater, often devastating, and even life-threatening. There are characteristics of adult children of abusive or dysfunctional families that countless people could benefit and be freed from, and that certainly includes Christians. That's what's so amazing about God's faithfulness as we trust Him.

I personally believe there is an enemy of the soul most often called the devil and named Satan. As one commits their life to God through Jesus Christ a battle begins and continues for our spiritual well-being and growth. The Word of God contains many scriptures about the existence of said enemy but many Christians deny that concept. One might ask, "Then why become a Christian and subject one's self to the battle?" My personal answer for that question is there's a void in our body and mind that only the love of God can fill even though there are perhaps billions who try to deny that essential need and fill that void with many other people, places, and things. As we attempt to grow stronger in our knowledge and relationship with God and Jesus Christ, the enemy knows exactly where and when to attack us. For many of us, including me, those attacks were based upon my struggle with wounded emotions, self-destructive habits, and negative self-images. Thanks be to God for His promise in I Thessalonians 5:23 to sanctify (make us holy and whole) in spirit, soul, and body. Verse 24 goes on to say the one who calls us is faithful and He *will do* as He promises. I'm a living witness to that transformation process that continues in me day by day.

Low self-esteem was a huge issue for me as a wounded child who never felt loved or worthy of love based on my parents' treatment. Also, I developed the thought pattern that anything less than perfect was unacceptable. That thinking led me to an unending sense of being a failure. Caretaking of others became my demise because I subconsciously craved esteem and approval from others rather than from God and myself. I had little to no knowledge in regard to the concepts of good health and nutrition. This in turn created much disdain for myself not being able to successfully overcome my weaknesses of sugar addiction, compulsive overeating, and emotional binging. Allow me today to gratefully say God has truly fulfilled so many promises in regard to making me whole and delivering me from those weaknesses according to my obedience and willingness to trust Him.

I could never seem to negate the deep-seated description of my being a "big ugly black bastard" that I certainly heard hundreds of times. I can still remember how each of those words singly sent what seemed like stabs in my heart! The incredible news is God attempted to remove that description in a most tangible way. My daughter, Tonya, and I were in the attic when we came upon my yearbook from high school and found my senior picture. She immediately got her eighth grade picture and compared the two. Her response was, "Mom! Look how much we look alike!" I instantly burst into tears as I realized it was nothing but God's healing grace that initiated that moment. I had never even thought of telling Tonya about that terrible name and my accompanying thoughts. It was so shameful as well as painful I had only shared it with a therapist and Ernie. There is absolutely no question that God, in his faithfulness, erased that terrible self-image. He saw fit to give me a new visual self-image in my renewed mind and assure me there was a great resemblance between myself and Tonya (who was absolutely gorgeous even then). I certainly had told her that I prayed specifically for a pretty girl but I had never made any association with our likenesses. Prior to that event I always thought my senior picture had been "doctored" and my complexion was obviously lightened.

Nancy & Tonya

As I enter into my senior season of life I've become well aware of the physical damage to my body that is a direct result of my child-hood trauma and my reactions to said trauma. The phenomenon is often referred to as the fight or flight physiological response that occurs in one's body and actually diminishes its ability to produce appropriate chemical responses to extremely stressful situations. I've certainly read about the physical effects of trauma but never real-ized how much of a cumulative effect they play havoc on our bodies for decades. Many of my present health conditions are the result of chemical imbalances that have depleted my body's ability to rebound from stress.

Today I've been blessed by God to realize that others originally generated these imbalances and I had absolutely no control over the circumstances. Many of my health issues are based on my inability to live beyond my addictive nature toward compulsive and unhealthy eating. The blessing is in the acknowledgement without self-condemnation that there are consequences to unacceptable habits and behaviors. Romans 8:1 assures believers there is no condemnation to those who are in Christ Jesus. The Holy Spirit within us delivers us from condemnation and produces a sense of spiritual rightness. Another great blessing is knowing I am not alone in this battle. The battle itself becomes a blessing in that I've been blessed with acknowledgement rather than denial of my brokenness.

I firmly believe once we commit our way to Jesus and reveal our hurts, the more we will then be healed. That thought is confirmation of what Paul says in Philippians 1:6, "Being confident of this, that he who began a good work in you will carry it on to completion until the day of Christ Jesus." I compare my emotional compulsive eating to the thorn in the flesh that Paul speaks of in 2 Corinthians 12. Paul, such a mighty warrior of Jesus Christ who demonstrated divine healing was unable to heal himself of whatever his infirmity may have been. I choose to believe it doesn't matter what the thorn might have been. Even though Paul asked God three times to remove said thorn God's wise and loving response was no! Verse 9 reads, "My grace is sufficient for you, for my power is made perfect in weakness." My thorn requires me to seek God's power on a daily and sometimes meal by meal basis and for that I'm actually grateful.

I experienced the harshest example of what could result from damaged emotions from my brother who chose not to live a life committed to God and Jesus Christ. He struggled for years with his addictions to marijuana, heroin, and alcohol. We both started smoking cigarettes early in our teen years and Doug was never able to kick that habit. I smoked intermittently for decades with several years of cessation at a time. However, when I wasn't smoking I was eating compulsively. Absolutely nothing but the grace of God has delivered me from self-destruction.

Doug was not as fortunate even though I was with him in church when he accepted Jesus as his Savior at age fifty-five. He never availed himself to studying God's word and discovering God's unconditional love. We did experience several years of togetherness after his last incarceration. However, over the years his addictions seemed to creep back into his life. He experienced a most devastating loss as a father when his nineteen-year-old son was shot and killed. I'll never forget the alarming phone call I received from Doug hysterically crying and asking me to come immediately to pick him up. As we approached the crime scene, I could not believe the indifference shown by the police, the coroner, as well as the bystanders. It was as if they were watching a drama on a television show rather than the brutal killing of a young man. The funeral was like nothing Doug and I had ever seen as gang members placed alcohol, cigarettes, drug paraphernalia, clothing, and tennis shoes in his casket. I can't begin to imagine the devastation Doug must have felt. Perhaps that was the beginning of his final surrender to emotional distress. His downward spiral ended on April 1, 2008, when he committed suicide by jumping off the Homestead Bridge in Pittsburgh, Pennsylvania. I choose to trust he received peace in his soul and eternal life.

Exalted

REFLECTION

My entire concept of being exalted is an expression of God himself lifting me above my derogatory life circumstances to a new level of faith and trust. Grateful doesn't begin to express my gratitude for His personal transformation in my regard. It would be totally impossible for me to continue to share without expressing the power God's word has instilled in me. I have experienced a renewing in the spirit mind that's spoken of in Ephesians 4:23. I must admit that many times I became discouraged when I realized that the old thoughts were often revisited and acted upon, but I came to believe what's written in Hebrews 6:4–6. That passage states that "It is impossible for those who have once been enlightened, who have tasted the heavenly gift, who have shared in the Holy Spirit, who have tasted the goodness of the word of God . . . if they fall away will be brought back to repentance." Thanks be to God that I came to realize that my transformation was not instant, but sure, based on my personal experiences and my willingness to study, trust, and believe God's word! Allow me to share some of the details of my journey toward exaltation through God's power and love. It is my specific prayer that you be blessed and encouraged to continue your journey through Jesus Christ our Lord and Savior and God's Holy Spirit within each of us! The passages of scripture I share have become much more than just words, but rather a part of my very being. I can say with complete assurance I agree with the apostle Paul when he says, "Being confident of this, that He who *began* a good work in you will carry it on to completion" (Philippians 1:6).

CHAPTER 18

Something More

As I continued to write and trust God in this memoir endeavor, I began to compare my walk with the Lord to the forty-year wilderness experience of God's people in the Old Testament. They, like me, had been repeatedly delivered from terrible circumstances. They, like me, had been given wondrous blessings time and time again but still lacked the total trust God yearned for from them (and me). From all the previous chapters God's numerous blessings and faithfulness were more than evident yet I was acutely aware of the painful emotional wounds I still carried from my traumatic childhood. So very many times I found myself acting and reacting to various adult situations in the present as if I were that abused little child again. When I wasn't acting or reacting I had the unending struggle with critical parent thoughts in my mind.

My initial and rather consistent reaction to strong emotional situations (good or bad) was to compulsively overeat. Even though I had been in and out of Overeaters Anonymous for at least thirty years and had certainly experienced growth and healing, compulsive overeating was still a stronghold in my life. I developed the awareness that sugar was my drug of choice and I had been a functional addict most of my adult life long after any other person was abusing me. There were certainly periods of time that I was able to experience physical abstinence and healthy eating, but many underlying defects of character remained and subsequently sabotaged my short successes. Adult Children of Alcoholics, Overeaters Anonymous, Alcoholics Anonymous, as well as group and individual therapy for years offered much clarity to my brokenness but I began to realize for certain that only God could completely eradicate my wounded spirit. It became quite evident that God wasn't finished with me yet.

What I failed to recognize was the extent of the addiction that might have been genetic as well as circumstantial. Today I recognize that from age twenty-five to sixty-five God was transforming me little by little as I continued to seek and trust Him. I have come to visualize my "spirit being" as a house with many rooms. God is so personal He examined my mind and spirit being and faithfully began a healing process in the rooms of my "heart house" that needed cleansed the most. In hindsight I realize that He was constantly permitting circumstances in order to teach me to trust Him. I imagine myself like the explanation God gave David in Psalm 32:8 of stubborn animals. God says, "Do not be like the horse or the mule, which has no understanding but must be controlled by bit and bridle or they will not come to you." That certainly describes me in my spiritual walk. I was stubborn and had extreme difficulty learning to trust God. Much of that lack of trust was based on the fact that I was never able to trust my earthly parents for not even basic survival needs.

Emotional weight is the heaviest and toughest to conquer. The issue of my mother's constant abandonment suggested to me that even God didn't love me and I was unlovable. I actually had a vision of my adult self carrying a huge garbage bag full of damaged emotions. As if that wasn't enough, I had critical voices that taunted me constantly about how little I mattered. I had deep thoughts that invaded my mind and strongly suggested I would never be good enough for anything! I continued to recognize that my recovery and healing was a process. I certainly had that concept in my head as I had said and heard it probably hundreds of times. However, my recovery and healing required a renewing of my spirit as well as my mind. What a revelation it was to realize that my recovery went far beyond the physical cravings and tendencies to overeat. I recognized God's faithfulness and personal healing that actually evolved over many years. It often appeared that nothing was changing but I know

today He was there all the time. The addictive tendencies and resulting self-destruction could have been so much worse even to a life
of crime, imprisonment, or death. Today, I can actually approach
God with thanksgiving for my food addiction that led me, by His
grace, to a personal relationship with Him that continues to grow
stronger and stronger as I study and apply His Word in my life. He
transformed me from feeling totally unloved and unlovable to experiencing His matchless and unconditional love. I have a moment-by-
moment awareness of how dependable and unfailing He is to me as
His *child*. Today, I'm constantly overwhelmed by the unquestionable,
genuine love I receive from others as yet another demonstration of
His love. I'm finally beginning to love myself in the same way I've
loved my neighbors for decades. *That's exalted!*

CHAPTER 19

My Dearest Mother

I never thought I would honestly be describing my mother as dearest. My true feelings were the exact opposite and would likely have been more appropriately expressed as my hated mother. I never gave myself permission to entertain those hateful thoughts for more than a few moments because they were just too shameful. I remember a time that I was called to come pick her up at a police station in the middle of the night. As a widow I felt I had little choice than to pack my young children in the car and proceed to that station. When I arrived the only word to describe what I felt was devastation.

My mother was so obviously drunk I nearly had to lift her frail body into the car. The stench from alcohol and urine was so strong I had to wind down all the windows in midwinter and expose my children to the cold air. I found myself praying that my children would fall asleep and believe that horrible experience was a dream when they woke up. I'm quite sure my mother recognized my disdain even in her drunken state. My negative thoughts were rampant as I drove to the place where she was currently living. It was a neighborhood where I didn't feel safe and I had no intention of getting out to walk her to the door. When she got out of the car and attempted to walk across the street, I saw another car approaching and for a few seconds I wished the car would hit and kill her!

I had never acknowledged to myself or anyone else that I had occasionally wished my mother were dead. After the incident I just described, my mother and I became estranged for two to three years. During that time my guilt became so intense I had to literally run out of church one Mother's Day. I had no idea whether my mother was dead or alive and the emotional pain was disheartening. Thank God I was in therapy at the time and my therapist skillfully led me through that crisis. She forced me to acknowledge the rage I had for my mother but had been able to repress because it seemed so very shameful and contradictory to my Christian beliefs.

On a subsequent session my therapist instructed me to use a padded bat to attack a sofa that represented my mother! That experience may sound despicable but it was extremely healing for me at age thirty-eight to finally give myself permission to begin to release that anger. Anger was a feeling I never outwardly expressed and had a very distorted opinion of. I'm grateful to this day for the wisdom and direction God gave my therapist to help me begin to resolve this major issue that had been so extremely damaging to my emotional and spiritual well-being. Releasing that pent up rage catapulted me into much needed awareness as I mentally processed some truths about my mother and her life circumstances. I realize how impossible it was to even begin to forgive my mother with all that rage. God began to graciously lead me to the understanding that only He can give. I have a personal note from around that same time in Proverbs 4:4 where Solomon instructs us to "Lay hold of my words with all your heart." Verse 5 goes on to say, "Get wisdom, get understanding." The peace I began to receive was just as Paul wrote about in Philippians 4:7. Paul was physically imprisoned, but I was mentally imprisoned. Along with that peace I surely did receive understanding! *That's exalted.* I began to be blessed with a new vision as follows.

My mother was a product of an abusive and dysfunctional family. It was an established fact that she received little to no emotional nurturing from her stepmother or father. In addition, she experienced strict discipline as a child and extreme control as a teenager. She must have been afraid all the time and angry most of the time. There was little to no affection demonstrated between her stepmother and father as husband and wife. Her birth mother died during childbirth when my mother was still an infant. My grandfather had become a widower with five young children. I'm told his second marriage was based upon convenience as he took an unwed mother as his wife and caretaker of his children. The result of that union was a terrible lack of knowledge and awareness regarding healthy marriage and parenting to my mother. Nurturing was undoubtedly a total void in her early years.

Mother was nineteen years old when she became pregnant with me. She was either uncertain of or in denial about her baby's father. Prior to her pregnancy, her siblings tell me that she had lots of drive, initiative, and personal motivation. More than anything she had a strong desire for acceptance and love. I can only imagine the dilemma she found herself in trying to decide which life issue was more important to her that might bring her the fulfillment she so desired. As much as she wanted success she also wanted to love and be loved. I'm certainly grateful for her decision to continue the pregnancy.

Marriage to the man I chose to believe was my father presented even more unfavorable consequences in my mother's young life. Very early in the marriage my "father" was emotionally unavailable and therefore the exact opposite of what my mother so desperately needed. She had no choice but to experience discouragement, disillusion, and disappointment. Today, I'm quite certain she did the best she could for as long as she could even though once again there was a terrible void in her life circumstances and basic human needs.

Unfortunately, it wasn't long before disappointments became overpowering and she began her pursuit of love and happiness with unfaithfulness to her marriage vows. I was four months old when Mommy realized she was pregnant again! The results of that pregnancy were further described in the chapter about my brother.

When she started to leave our family for months at a time she probably got caught up in an obsessive desire for the excitement of new relationships and sexual encounters. I remember her admitting to me during a few weeks of rehab and sobriety that the only attention she got from her father was physical abuse, scolding, and punishment. She never experienced healthy love in her home environment and probably struggled mentally from deeply ingrained childhood thoughts that strongly suggested love was demonstrated by abuse.

After the romance subsided in all of these encounters, she sought distorted attention from physical beatings. It was as if she had a desire to be punished for her inappropriate behaviors.

After years of alcoholism and physical abuse, my mother's entire countenance changed. Her nose showed evidence of being broken perhaps several times to the point it was actually crooked. Her lips were distended and had visible scars from having been repeatedly split open. She eventually was declared legally blind based on the damage from repeated eye injuries. Even the thick eyeglasses she was forced to wear were frequently broken and taped in the middle. Her life situation spiraled downward as she continued to become involved with less than desirable men. Her disease progressed to the point she found herself reunited with my "father" and even from him occasional beatings persisted. Unfortunately, my mother's husband became terminally ill and deceased from cancer of the lung with distant metastases in 1979 at age fifty-six. My mother was fifty-two at the time of her husband's death.

The last eight years of Mommy's life could only be considered pitiful even though her sister Lella remained devoted to her regardless of her choices for companionship and destructive behavior. I surmise today the reason for Aunt Lella's compassion was not only based on the good person she was, but also because she knew my mother's secret truth. I'm also sure my mother's brothers knew of her demise, but chose to keep silent. I would spend time on holidays as my mom visited Aunt Lella, but I seldom took my children because I chose not for them to see their grandmother's state.

In addition to poor companionship, my brother had become seriously addicted again to heroin and leaned heavily on my mother for cash when she had it from social security or her deceased husband's pension. There were occasions when he, too, beat my mother as she reluctantly refused to give him her money. There was even one occasion my mother called me, frightened nearly to death, from a nearby store to tell me Doug had locked her out of her apartment! When I arrived I had a knife and every intention to use it if my brother threatened me. I got him to leave as I threatened to call the police, but I was barely in my car to leave when my mother was calling him back and apologizing for putting him in danger. Needless to say, I resolved to distance myself from both of them when I realized the risk I had taken.

On April 1, 1987, I was in Philadelphia, Pennsylvania for some job training when I was called out of class. I was told I had to fly to Pittsburgh immediately. I insisted on calling my children to check on them. When they told me they were okay I thought perhaps someone was pulling an April fool's joke on me. However, a work associate who was also in the class made arrangements for us to fly back to Pittsburgh and my work location. I still thought this was a terrible joke, but my boss strongly urged me to call Citizen's Hospital in New Kensington based upon a call they had received from someone who said he was my brother. I knew then it was probably something to do with my mom and I was angry to say the least that again my job performance was being affected by her negligent lifestyle. On many previous occasions I would receive calls from police stations or hospitals to come rescue her.

I couldn't believe what I was hearing when the hospital employee said they had been wondering when someone was finally going to call in regard to my mother's tragic death! Needless to say, I rushed to the hospital only to be informed of the distressing details of my mother's death. Apparently, my brother had coaxed my extremely sick mother out of bed to accompany her to the bank and cash her check for his drug money. As they returned to my mother's apartment building, she told my brother she needed to rest before she negotiated a very steep flight of steps. In his haste for his drug, my brother left my mother sitting on the steps where she unfortunately slumped over and died. My brother returned to see an ambulance and was told by neighbors what had happened. His reaction was to leave the scene once he found out her body would be taken to the hospital and call me on my job.

I still don't have the words to describe the myriad of emotions I experienced, but I immediately jumped into action to notify the funeral home and suppress my feelings. Thank God I knew my mother had insurance because I paid it once yearly. My brother tearfully and apologetically called me a day or so later and I prayerfully invited him to come to the funeral home to be involved in the arrangements. He never took advantage of that opportunity but to this day I'm glad I asked. When he showed up for the funeral he was obviously high and the church service was already over. Soon afterward, he was again incarcerated and we totally lost touch. What remains ironic and sad is my brother committed suicide on April 1 (the same day of my mother's death) in 2008. I will always have to wonder how strongly Doug was influenced on that date. I was informed that he possibly had relapsed and was using heroin again. My heart still aches for him because I know his truth. The losses of his son and his mother, in addition to his demon addiction, were just too overwhelming for him without God's help.

So ends the many circumstances of my mother's life struggles. I absolutely thank God for the total forgiveness, compassion, and genuine love that accompany my thoughts of her today. There but for the grace of God go I if my addiction had been something other than food. *That's exalted!*

Mommy

CHAPTER 20

Spiritual Understanding

My progression to feelings of total forgiveness, compassion, and genuine love was a process administered by God himself on my behalf
as I continued to trust *in* Him and *on* Him. Allow me to share the
very beginning of that process as I wrote the following letter to my
mother two days after her death. I was strongly led to arrive early at
the funeral home to be able to actually read it to her from my spirit
to hers.

April 3, 1987

Dear Mommy,

It's really true you're dead. I hurt because
you're dead. I'm relieved because you're dead. I'll
no longer have to physically detach myself from
you to escape the pain of watching you destroy
yourself as an alcoholic. That hurt longer than I
can even remember. But you know, Mommy, I
understand more today and recently about your
disease of alcoholism.

I understand that it was a physical addiction
that was the result of emotional unrest that you
probably had all your life for whatever reasons. I

understand, you see, because the same thing has happened to me with food over the past twenty-five years even though it didn't show until about the last fifteen years. Because I'm searching for answers for myself I have come to understand more about how hard it was for you to stop your self-destructive behavior. I, too, have become caught up in that same self-destruction with my eating behaviors.

That understanding, however, does not remove the hurt I feel for your actions toward me and it doesn't remove the anger either. I suppose only time, more healing, my forgiveness, and God's love and strength will replace that hurt. I'm glad I don't have to be hurt anymore. I'm glad your struggle is over. I pray that I will always remember that I have been and could be the same without the help and recovery I'm seeking today by the grace of God. You know, Mommy, I've even been able lately to be glad for the bad times I had as a child because even though I have emotional scars, I realize the end result hasn't been and doesn't have to be all bad for me. It's a life lesson, an example of what could happen to me and a rude awakening in regard to my need of continued emotional and spiritual healing.

Thank you, Mommy, for doing your best when you could. I'm slowly moving toward not blaming you anymore and now that you're gone, I intend to go on toward recovery, forgiving, loving, and growing into the fullness of life that God intended for me. There are no more roadblocks except me and the ones I put on myself. No more excuses. No more unresolved mother love issue and hope for it. It's on to the full love of God and myself that I've longed for from you and others all my life. Yes, Mommy, IT'S ABOUT ME NOW!

Thank you for the love you gave. Thank you for the love you couldn't and didn't give. Thank you for my physical life. I forgive you. I love you and always will. I hated the things you did but I know I didn't hate YOU. If I had hated you, I would not have hurt so much as I watched you destroy yourself over the years.

I hope this letter of love will leave you and me in peace and with love. Look down from heaven and pray for me and my needed emotional healing and recovery from my disease.

Love, Nancy

Several months after my mother's death I had a very specific experience that took place at a retreat for adult children of alcoholics. All the participants were outwardly successful African-American professionals. The facilitators directed us to role play certain situations as if they were happening in the present. My specific incident was someone lying on the floor covered with a sheet and a liquor bottle held close to the chest. My instructions were to talk to my deceased mother and share my deepest thoughts and emotions that I had never verbally expressed. Needless to say, that incident was extremely intense but absolutely crucial for my continued recovery.

After the incident of having a discussion with my deceased mother, I was instructed to meditate and then write a letter expressing the same feelings that I had in that role playing session. I certainly had read God's word in Proverbs 3:5 that instructs us to "lean not on our own understanding." I had accepted that concept in my head but struggled with it in my spirit for decades. "Why?" was a prevalent question that I often asked God. I know today that God was preparing me to receive that understanding in His time, not mine. God has fulfilled His promise of the Holy Spirit gift of discernment that leads to a keener wisdom according to His divine plan for me as His child. *That's exalted!*

I prayed with great earnestness and followed the instructions to write about my thoughts and conversation to my deceased mother. It was so healing and affirming to have been totally truthful especially in the presence of other people. The shame seemed to have been resolved as I began to write the following.

August 1987

Dear Mommy,

As I've grown older and experienced more of life's realities, I've also come to understand more about the results of certain life circumstances. I've grown to accept more of the "unfavorable" circumstances of my life and to be a lot less judgmental of the people involved. I trust you'll accept this letter as an expression of love from me to you.

I must honestly say that for many years of my life I "felt" little love for you based on the hurt from the many disappointments I had in our relationship. The hate seemed so much stronger than what little love I could seem to muster up for a few fleeting moments at a time. Today I've come to understand that love is not just a feeling. It can also be a deep appreciation of someone. One thing I *know* is that I *always wanted* to love you and always wanted that love to be returned.

I've spent much time actually searching for signs of your love for me. My love for you begins with the fact that you chose to have me and give me life itself. I love you for trying very hard in my early childhood years to make that time as wonderful as you could for me. I don't remember those times but today I accept other people's remembrances. I love you for your encouragement and praises in my adult years as I married, became a good wife and mother, and achieved a successful career. I love you for the pride you demonstrated about me in your sober times. I received that pride as a blessing and a symbol of your love for me in what I had become as an adult in spite of our histories.

I cannot say I loved you for leaving me right when I felt I needed you the most during puberty and adolescent stages. Those were very painful, lonely, and embarrassing years for me. It was a struggle to understand how you could love me and yet constantly leave as well as emotionally, verbally, and physically abuse me. I do see now that your childhood circumstances left you with little hope and strength to give to another human being. I believe also that you were very guilt-ridden and had difficulties of your own from unresolved emotional issues. Unfortunately, those issues were a battle you fought but lost.

Please know that my present issues and many past ones have brought me to a greater understanding of your actions and reactions. You see, I, too, am fighting that same battle and often wonder how successful I'm doing at it. On the surface and to the outside world I appear to be handling my life problems, but inside I know that it's a hell of a battle that I too often think about surrendering. The result of my struggles is a much greater appreciation for you as well as acceptance of the love void I "felt." I know you loved me, Mommy, I know you wanted a good life for me that you weren't able to produce so it seemed. But you know what, Mommy? You perhaps had some unrealistic expectations of your-self as a mother that God (the real director of our lives) honored and blessed me with by His matchless grace.

I could have shown some thankfulness for your desires for me as an adult woman. I have those same desires for my children but I've come to realize that I (like you) am only partly respon-sible for the fulfillment of those desires. More and more responsibility becomes theirs as they grow older and make their own life choices. Finally, I'm grateful for even a small concept of uncon-ditional love. That's what I've grown to have for you, Mommy, little by little and I trust you'll accept that love even in your physical absence. It is truly and finally given from me to you based on the love I'm receiving from God.

Love Always,
Nancy

At that point in my spiritual journey I truly understood not only in words but in my very spirit the anointing I had received when I was totally able to do as Paul advised in Philippians 3:13, "This one thing I do, forgetting those things which are behind, and reaching forth unto those things which are before." Paul certainly had his rea-sons to forget who he was and what he did before his salvation. My personal application of that passage was a very long and different process. Little did I know for myself how impossible it was to totally "forget" the anguish of my childhood without complete forgiveness. My inner healing required total surrender of the emotional pain that had been a stronghold in my life for decades. Today I remember the events with a totally new vision that enables me to indeed move on according to God's plan and specific purpose for me. I totally agree with Paul who writes in Philippians 1:6, "Being confident of this very thing, that He who has begun a good work in you will perform it until the day of Jesus Christ." Thank God I'm a work in progress!

The spiritual maturity through God and Jesus Christ surely enables me to receive the fullness spoken of in the Bible. My mind has certainly been renewed and more than ever, I am a new creature. Finally, old things had truly passed and all things became new! *That's exalted!*

CHAPTER 21

My Truth

Biblestudytools.com lists 469 times the word *truth* is mentioned. I have prayerfully chosen only a few that are especially relevant for my written testimony. It would be impossible for me to share my personal truth without scripture references. Even as I write this important chapter, I've been on my knees and prostrate on my face trusting God for His anointing that the words might touch those who desperately need it and therefore receive healing as I have. I cannot begin to count the times I've heard "the truth will set you free." I selectively chose the truths I wanted to admit to myself, and not even think about mentioning to others! I'm certain there are nonbelievers as well as genuine believers of the word of God who are in total denial of many of their personal truths. As a member of many support and Bible study groups over many years, my truth evolved little by little as God's plan for me unfolded.

In John 8:31–32 the words of Jesus are recorded, "If you hold to my teaching, you are really my disciples. Then you will know the truth and the truth will set you free." I can't begin to describe the power and transformation that I've experienced from these passages. They will never be just words to me but rather an established fact that resides deep in my spirit. Please note, however, the condition for us to receive the blessings of these and all passages is that we hold to Jesus's teachings. In Psalm 51:6 repentant David says to the Lord, "Surely you desire truth in the inner parts." Jesus promised in

John 15:26 that God would send a counselor (the Holy Spirit) as our source for truth. John 16:13 goes further by declaring, "But when he the Spirit of truth comes he will guide you into all truth." When Jesus was questioned about how believers would know the way after He departed, He answered in John 14:6, "I am the way, the Truth, and the life."

Those are all amazing scriptures full of power for all of us who believe. Allow me please to put my personal spin on them. For as long as I can remember I would hear my mother shout in her rages that the man I called my father was not! Yes, I heard it, but I chose not to believe it. I also attempted not to believe that I was the cause of all her life problems. I could never understand my mother's apparent inability to love me until I learned the real circumstances of my conception. The truth is, my mother was a victim of incest and I was the product of one of those horrible experiences. For the sake of my remaining family members, I will not share the details, but God in His faithfulness delicately led me to my truth. I remember perhaps in 1986 during a time my mother was in rehab, I begged her to tell me the truth. She only would admit that the man I called father was not, but it would be best if I not know who really was. I was certainly disappointed but I could obviously see how emotionally painful this subject seemed to be for her.

Many years later, in 1987, after Mommy was deceased God himself permitted me to be given the truth. I had just returned from a retreat where I had role played to my mother's corpse, prayed, and wrote my letter. As God would have it, I received a God-incidence (not coincidence) call from my mother's closest childhood friend and I was led to ask her who my father actually was. Her response at that time was, if my mother had wanted me to know she would have told me. It was still painful for me as I continued to grieve my mother's death and my unresolved birth issue. My therapist suggested I purchase a baby doll that would, by suggestion, be me and I could re-parent myself. I actually benefited from loving that doll but my unresolved issue remained painful. In 2011, when I committed to writing this memoir, I had a strong desire to contact my mom's childhood friend again, but I didn't even know if she was still alive. I also was fearful that she would again refuse to give me the information I was seeking. I prayed several times but never got the courage to seek her out. Somehow I knew my truth was needed to heal my wounded inner self but my fear of the truth seemed greater.

Once again as God would have it, I was in a store and heard someone call my name. It was indeed the woman I had wanted to reach! Another God-incidence! We agreed to have lunch and some more prayers were offered up. When I took this wonderful woman home, I courageously asked her again about my birth father and thanks be to God she reluctantly shared the truth with me. Needless to say, the pain from that revelation left a very heavy burden on my heart and I must have cried for weeks. However, the eventual blessing was as I continued to write this memoir seeking God's direction, He faithfully provided memory after memory and along with them the freedom He promises in the truth. Many times I had to stop writing for days in order to emotionally process the revelations. I became aware that I truly was experiencing peace and much understanding. God also slowly blessed me with compassion that I could never have imagined I'd ever experience in relation to my childhood experiences and those who inflicted me with their damaging actions. *That's exalted!*

Just as God promised I became aware of countless thoughts and wisdoms that could only be described as divinely inspired. I knew those experiences were directly from God based upon how personal they were in my regard. Just as John spoke of in Chapter 16:13, God's Holy Spirit within my spirit guided me from truth to truth. There was no other conclusion for me but to totally acknowledge the fact that Jesus was indeed the way who gave me my truth and a totally transformed life. It is my sincere prayer that those of you who I've been blessed to share this life-changing experience might boldly seek God for your truth that will set you free from emotional strongholds that hinder you from receiving all that is offered us through Jesus Christ. You, too, can press on to attain personal knowledge and healing in your mind, body, and spirit.

I've found through much research that I fit into a very specific and well defined group of adults who have been categorized as victims based upon childhood trauma. The group name is ACE, which is described as Adverse Childhood Experiences. Discovery of this nationally acclaimed group was yet another blessing from God to assure me I was by no means alone. Perhaps some of you who have not begun a life journey walking with God and Jesus Christ will still begin a search for your "something more" and pursue a life that consists of more than just existing day to day with pain from decades before. I strongly encourage you to search the Internet. At that site perhaps millions of others can find for information about ACE. The following is my short summarization of the ACE score concept and a way to calculate where you might fit in a score from one to ten. The higher the ACE score, the greater the risk of experiencing poor physical and mental health, and negative social consequences later in life. The questions are as follows:

Finding Your ACE Score
While you were growing up, during your first eighteen years of life:

1. Did a parent or other adult in the household often or very often . . . Swear at you, insult you, put you down, or humiliate you? Or Act in a way that made you afraid that you might be physically hurt?
    If yes enter 1 _____
2. Did a parent or other adult in the household often or very often . . . push, grab, slap, or throw something at you? or ever hit you so hard that you had marks or were injured?
    If yes enter 1 _____
3. Did an adult person at least 5 years older than you ever... Touch or fondle you or have you touch their body in a sexual way? or Attempt or actually have oral, anal, or vaginal intercourse with you?
    If yes enter 1 _____
4. Did you often or very often feel that . . . No one in your family loved you or thought you were important or special?

or Your family didn't look out for each other, feel close to each other, or support each other?
If yes enter 1 _____

5. Did you often or very often feel that . . . You didn't have enough to eat, had to wear dirty clothes, and had no one to protect you? or Your parents were too drunk or high to take care of you or take you to the doctor if you needed it?
If yes enter 1 _____

6. Were your parents ever separated or divorced?
If yes enter 1 _____

7. Was your mother or stepmother: Often or very often pushed, grabbed, slapped, or had something thrown at her? or Sometimes, often, or very often kicked, bitten, hit with a fist, or hit with something hard? or Ever repeatedly hit at least a few minutes or threatened with a gun or knife?
If yes enter 1 _____

8. Did you live with anyone who was a problem drinker or alcoholic or who used street drugs?
If yes enter 1 _____

9. Was a household member depressed or mentally ill, or did a household member attempt suicide?
If yes enter 1 _____

10. Did a household member go to prison?
If yes enter 1 _____

Now add up your "Yes" answers: _____ This is your ACE Score.

I will lovingly share with you my score is 9+! I chose not to totally count my mentally ill "uncle" that was permanently hospitalized from syphilis but often was released for thirty-day visits. Awareness of my high risk factor actually produced an even more profound sense of gratitude to God for His many touches in my life. A mere comparison of my brother and myself shows the difference in our lives, his ending at age fifty-nine from suicide and my two failed suicide attempts. What I know for sure is there's an absolute connection between ACE scores and long-term adult physical conditions. The higher the score the higher the likelihood of some of the following health conditions also referred to on the CDC/ACE site such as:

Alcoholism	COPD	Depression
Fetal Death	Illicit Drug Use	Ischemic heart disease
Liver Disease	Smoking	Suicide attempts
Sexually transmitted disease		

There are also quality of life issues that are prevalent such as:

Poor work performance	Financial stress
Intimate partner violence	Multiple sexual partners
Unintended pregnancies	Early sexual activity
Adolescent pregnancy	Risk for sexual violence
Poor academic achievement	

My prayer is that your spiritual healing begins or continues with awareness even from this ACE information. There certainly has been recovery from all of the above DIS-eases in 12-Step groups and I personally thank God for mine. The fact is, two men who attended a Presbyterian Bible study group founded Alcoholics Anonymous, the very first group. My humble observation is, over the decades the biblical principles and the need for a personal relationship with the author of that Word who I still call God, not a higher power, has diminished. In many groups today, the Lord's Prayer has been eliminated. My personal experience was Christianity first, and according to God's faithfulness, I was led to 12-Step groups to continue His work in me. The steps as I came to understand them, are still extremely prevalent in my life because they are derived from powerful and life-changing scriptures. Each and every meeting and convention I attended were indeed touches from God supplying just what I needed at that particular time and place in my life.

It's difficult at this point for me to realize that my testimony has now been written and my truth has been revealed. The Lord has indeed placed a burden in my heart to reach out, with His direction, to others who are in dire need of similar touches. My prayer for all who read this testimony is that they be exalted or elevated above this life's many trials and tribulations. Jesus himself suffered many trials and said we would have them also. I've been graciously equipped to share my hope and encourage you to realize Jesus also said as much as possible to be of good cheer because we can indeed conquer the emotional demons in our life. I have already been blessed as Job was in the Bible in that God has blessed the latter part of my life more than the first part. *That's exalted!*

Thank you, God; thank you, Jesus; and thank you, Holy Spirit! Thank God for His amazing grace!

Epilogue

Praise God that I'm forever exalted above so very much!

I am God's child. He is and has been my Father.

I've studied God's word and totally accepted His Love.

The Holy Spirit has equipped me to receive emotional healing of my soul and spirit.

I'm exalted based on the renewal of my mind and as I continue to walk with God it is renewed day by day.

I've totally forgiven my mother and God has placed compassion in my heart for her.

I have respect for the man I called my father understanding now why even a little provision for me was difficult.

I'm even more grateful for the beloved woman I called Grandma and her love for me in spite of the truth.

God has given me understanding that many of my mother's drunken vicious attacks were actually directed at her abusers that I represented in the flesh.

My mother's deep-seated issues and damaged emotions were the result of her childhood abuse and for that I forgive and love her even more.

God has seen fit to deliver me and perhaps my children from many generational curses that plagued our ancestors.

I've been given God's power to resist my emotional triggers.

My emotional baggage is gone forever.

I'm released daily from the stronghold of compulsive overeating by God's matchless grace. Satan continues to tempt me but God has given me the power to overcome.

I'm grateful for the self-love God has given and the self-destructive habits He has removed. I am a new creature.

Today I fully recognize that God has a specific plan and purpose for me and the balance of my life that includes hope, success, and a future. Jeremiah 29:11.

Today I no longer live in constant guilt and shame from the physical appearance of my body. I've let go of those old thoughts and am grateful to be alive to tell and share my testimony and my "battle scars."

I realize my future is in God's hands and He has not given me a spirit of fear but rather a spirit of love and a sound, renewed mind (2 Timothy 1:7). *That's exalted!*

About the Author

Nancy was married to her now deceased husband for seventeen years. She's lived as a widow and single parent for thirty-four years. She worked twenty-nine years in telecommunications and retired as a trunk facilities engineer.

Today she lives in a suburb of Pittsburgh and enjoys her adult son and daughter's spouses and three wonderful grandchildren.

CPSIA information can be obtained
at www.ICGtesting.com
Printed in the USA
BVHW072026011118
531619BV00001B/5/P

9 781642 993202